A Playbook for
Reinventing Your Career
in a World That Won't
Stand Still

A Playbook for Reinventing Your Career in a World That Won't Stand Still

Elizabeth Bowker

IGUANA

Copyright © 2025 Elizabeth Bowker
Published by Iguana Books
720 Bathurst Street
Toronto, ON M5S 2R4

Publisher: Cheryl Hawley
Editor: Dana Sorensen
Front cover design: Joy Huang

ISBN 978-1-77180-743-2 (paperback)
ISBN 978-1-77180-744-9 (epub)

This is an original print edition of *A Playbook for Reinventing Your Career
in a World That Won't Stand Still.*

For Timothy Cuffe who has been instrumental in making this book happen and who has always taken such good care of my confidence.

Acknowledgements

I'm grateful to those who supported the research and writing of this book. First, I must thank my husband, Robert Jackes, for whom it is a vast understatement to say he has been steadfast in his support and encouragement. Second, I thank Marlisse Silver-Sweeney for her ever-present ear, sage advice, good humour and enduring friendship. And finally, I'm so grateful to all the many people I interviewed and spoke with in researching this book, about half of whose stories are included. Their willingness to speak openly and candidly about the ups and downs of their careers, as well as their hopes and their dreams, has been instrumental in my work and has inspired me greatly. They are each in the bones of this work.

Table of Contents

Part 1
Your Working Life

Introduction

CAREER IMAGINATION

What would you be doing if there were no limits, no doubts, no distractions? What makes you feel like you're doing the work you were meant to do? What does your ideal workday feel like? Imagine the sky at its bluest. This process of dreaming about what's possible for your career is known as "Career Imagination."[i] It starts with believing that your dream can come true, no matter who you are. You free yourself to consider all the options. You set goals that might have seemed impossible in the past. You start to feel like wonderful careers can happen to ordinary people, because they do — it's true — every day. Family responsibilities, health problems, or a lack of formal education can make it harder, but you can still get that really satisfying next job or new career. It might look different than you first thought. It might take a little longer than you would like. But in the end, the dream needs to fit you.

Once you've imagined the wonderful job of your dreams, you need a plan to make it real. Part of that planning is understanding the world you want to work in and the trends shaping that part of the labor market so that you head in a direction where employers are hiring and you have the skills they're looking for. A good plan will help you set a clear path with reduced risk. It should be tailored to you, your dreams, your values, and your family. In the end, you'll arrive at the right place with expectations and confidence to match the opportunity.

In my journey to learn more about what people want from work and how this might change over a lifetime, I interviewed more than a hundred people with a wide variety of experiences, and I learned what leads to career success for the ordinary person with an ordinary education — and usually some big dreams. I talked to people like you. People who need achievable strategies to get where they want to be, not fantastic advice that feels out of reach.

One of the first people I met with was Ava. She told me she'd worked as an accountant for years, but she was never really satisfied. She was also a passionate music fan who wasn't afraid to dream big about how she could make music into her career. She polished up her Career Imagination, putting a lot of thought into leaving a sure thing for a dream thing, and in the end, she did it. Ava left the firm and took a master's degree in music management in Manchester, UK. Today, she works in music promotion in London and has even done some producing. She's played a part in developing some of the best contemporary music on the planet in one of its most exciting cities. She meets with musicians, managers, and record labels and goes to some of the best concerts in the world. She still works with spreadsheets, but she's having a lot more fun. Ava dreamed it, and she did it.

When I interviewed Vaneese, I heard something familiar. After years of working in service jobs, she was ready for change. She said she wanted something more and had already imagined it — her own business selling perfume under her own name. She knows someone who can develop this for her, and she's learned what she needs to do for tax purposes, but she still needs to know more about the perfume market to sell and distribute her product. In the process, she might find a more suitable product that's in demand and that she understands. Vaneese needs a little more work on her dream and a more developed plan, but she's got some good Career Imagination going for her!

Ava and Vaneese both understand that dreams must be grounded in reality. We don't work in a vacuum. What's happening in the world around us affects what jobs are available, the quality of those jobs, and the likelihood of our professional success and satisfaction. The world right now is volatile and uncertain — you already know that. In the face of change, we adapt and, hopefully, better things follow. The good news here is that there's a lot you can do to direct your career so you can enjoy the work you want, when and where you want. We call this "decent" work, and everyone deserves it.

There's an age-old push and pull between employers and workers. That won't change, but it shifts and we adapt. Throughout the 20th century, workers gained more rights, better pay, more safety, and health benefits, and limited work hours and holidays. This was driven in part by the United Nations' 1948 *Declaration on Human Rights,* which, among other things, helped create the shared belief that everyone deserves plentiful and decent paid work. It means you can live comfortably and save for old age, but it's much more than that.

At its most basic, decent work means you control when and where you work, have time off to enjoy with your family and community, you're safe, and you can get better quality work if you want to. For some people, this means being self-employed, but there are many ways to work (and many ways to be self-employed). Gone are the days when the farm or the factory were your only options. Our aim is to set you up for decent work, and enough of it.

In the 21st century, we're gaining more flexibility and autonomy in our work. People are changing jobs more often and not settling for something just because they're already there. But independence comes at the price of greater risk, shifted from the employer to us. More of us work part-time or in some form of non-permanent work, like contracting, consulting, and gig work. When we work this way, we have less job security and fewer benefits, such as a pension, to fall back on. But it also means we're free to pursue independent work, such as freelancing, consulting, and contracting. All this contributes to how we *feel* about our jobs and our employers. Today, our relationship with work and employers is more fluid. On average, we're leaving jobs sooner and more often, and if you do switch jobs, it's easier than it used to be.

My colleague Tim had lived in Hong Kong for sixteen years when he and his wife made the life-altering decision to return to Canada with newborn twins. At the time, Tim held a high-paying senior communications role at a global investment bank, but they needed to be back with their families. Leaving that professional stability — along with a well-established network and reputation — was scary. He had to recalibrate, not just professionally, but personally. He had to exercise his Career Imagination, but he struggled with this at first. He didn't know what he was going to do. It pushed him to broaden his expertise beyond corporate communications into the world of marketing, brand strategy, and customer engagement. In the process, he learned that reinvention doesn't come with a road map — it comes from trusting your values, taking chances, and betting on yourself, even when the path is unclear. His next job was in marketing and communications leadership. It was a great job that broadened his skills and provided well for his family.

Inevitably, we'll be looking for work and adapting to new work repeatedly throughout our careers. And that means, more than ever, we need to be prepared to change jobs and gain new skills, a necessary trade-in for the greater satisfaction and reward in the new job. This goes better with a good plan, and I'll show you how to make one. Most people report being happier in their work one year after a job change. So that part is fun, especially if you like change. If you don't like change, you can reduce stress and risk by having a good plan and a better idea of what's coming your way. Uncertainty can be scary, but with careful thought, you can prepare for what's next.

For most of us, good work is meaningful and gives us a sense of doing something valuable, especially if it's helpful to other people. But not everyone has that in their life. In this book, we'll examine the current and future environment of work, not from a management or policy perspective, but from the view of who you are when you go to work so that you too can enjoy good work.

Over the next several chapters, this book will help you make a sound plan tailored to you: your experience, your desires, and your strengths. We'll look at the world we all work in because where you work and who you work with will influence how satisfied you are in your job and how well it works for you. But also, to get the work you want, it's helpful to understand the bigger picture: What's shaping the future of work and influencing your industry? What are the labor trends, and which skills do you need? Which jobs are in demand, and what do you need to do to get from where you are to where you dream of being?

These influences are like the currents beneath the surface of your career path, sometimes pushing you forward and other times pulling you in unexpected directions. To navigate them, it's helpful to see what's coming and to understand the changes reshaping industries, roles, and opportunities. If you choose work that is less in demand, you can plan accordingly, knowing it might be a little harder to find.

As you weave your way through this book, you'll find lots of action items. I encourage you to get a notebook and create your own "Career Imagination Journal." Or you can use the workbook that accompanies this book. It provides a step-by-step plan to activate your Career Imagination and to draw a path to reshape your career.

I understand that there are very real constraints that make the changes you want more difficult to achieve. Limitations come to most of us at some point. As a sole guardian single mother, I had to choke on my ambition and work less than I wanted for close to twenty years while I put my children first. I didn't have to limit my career as much as I did, but hands-on was how I wanted to raise my kids. Once they were big, I was ready to get moving, and I did. In those twenty years, I could have hired more childcare or worked out an agreement with another parent in a similar position and focused more on my career, but it's not the choice I made. I waited to make my career changes and developed my Career Imagination — I really worked hard at that. Now I'm realizing my dreams by researching and writing more *and* becoming an entrepreneur.

Chapter One

BIG FACTORS & MEGA-TRENDS:

Finding Your Place

The things that shape the world and how we live in it also affect our work experience.[ii] Obviously, politics and the economy have major impacts on the labor market and conditions for those of us who work in it, but there's much more. People are living longer and becoming more educated. They're also moving around the globe more. New technologies and globalization have influenced and changed what jobs are available and how we do them. Employers are more aware of social issues like loneliness and general employee well-being.

Knowing about the big factors can help you make better decisions about your future — including how and where you want to work. Understanding how shifts in the world can affect your job means you'll be better able to adapt to those changes when they come to your workplace. It's good to keep in mind that even though these things push us around, people will power the future. We are key to unlocking the benefits of innovation and growth — they happen with us and the jobs we do.

I interviewed Tony, who adapted to changes in the world but also in himself. He was a forest firefighter who did exciting, dangerous, and important work. By 2020, the fires were getting more intense, he was getting older, and he didn't like the way some of the processes were becoming more bureaucratic. Besides, no one can be a flame jumper forever. In the off months, Tony put in a lot of thought, did some solid research and talked to a lot of people. He still wanted to work in the woods and keep using the skills he'd developed. His research led him to a job with an Indigenous tribe in their forest management services, helping with fire suppression tactics. Sometimes, he even gets to work with a few of his old crewmates. This work is more sustainable and perhaps even more effective in stopping the spread of wildfires. He also has the satisfaction of working for an organization that is forward-thinking even as it's rooted in traditional knowledge.

Technology & the Future of Jobs

While technology wasn't what motivated change for Tony, it's the single biggest driver of change in our working lives, now and in the past. Artificial intelligence (AI) is changing how we complete tasks, and from that, the way we work and the jobs we do; it's eliminating some jobs and creating others. E-commerce, cybersecurity, and big data are also areas for job growth and job change. These technological changes can be life changing, allowing more people to contribute to the workforce in ways that weren't allowed in the past. These technologies also mean fewer jobs in some areas and more in others.

Technology now allows many people to work remotely and to have opportunities to work in roles that weren't available to them before; this is especially true of people living away from large city centers and those with a disability, which made working in a traditional environment especially challenging. There are more people with disabilities working, and more understanding of what people with varied needs require to do their jobs. As work changes, there comes a demand for people with new skills in many places. For instance, climate change is driving the development of new technologies. As companies focus on sustainability, new jobs that use those technologies are being created.

You've heard and you've seen that technology is changing jobs and work, but to date, it's not been happening cataclysmically; it's more incremental. New technologies generally get integrated into existing systems rather than creating wholesale change. This should give you time to assess and consider where you may or may not fit in. Today, technological changes in our workplaces are driven by AI, big data, 3D printing, and robotics. New technologies are often integrated into existing systems, replacing repetitive tasks and freeing up workers to focus on more creative and complex aspects of their jobs. The good news is that the World Economic Forum and other experts suggest that new technologies will be net job creators sooner rather than later. Still, it must be said that the rate of change is unprecedented, and it's too early to make a firm prediction.

The new jobs created are likely to require specialized skills and may come with higher wages. We're not necessarily advocates for more formal education, but this is an example where upskilling could be beneficial to you. Many of these new jobs are in the United States, where big data has changed how we collect, track, and use information — mountains of information. Along with data comes investments in cybersecurity. And although employers everywhere are learning to use AI to create efficiencies, which has often resulted in job losses, it can also lead to the creation of new jobs in many sectors.

When I spoke with Keenan, an electrical engineer working in Intelligent Transportation Systems (ITS), a field that has already been transformed by AI, he told me that the next ten to fifteen years were going to be really exciting. But he also noted that he was having trouble finding experienced engineers with the right skills to fill his team. "I can get new people without much experience, but my challenge is to keep the older workers. I need their skills to work with these new complex problems. It takes $300,000 to train someone, so you don't just let them walk out the door." He now needs to hire and train for skills that didn't exist a decade ago, but someone looking forward could have anticipated what was going to happen in transportation and could have begun to develop those skills early. They still can.

Artificial Intelligence

AI has well and truly reached the workforce and changed it permanently. We've been using it for years to improve our grammar, sort data, make calculations, and better reach our customers. More recently, with the advent of generative AI, it's been used more widely for complex calculations, to write emails and documents, to enhance consumer interactions and as an idea generator. AI is also really good at coding and data analysis.

Firms are rapidly building AI capabilities in processes and digital products, and improvement is constant and dramatic. Currently, AI is a productivity booster, automating boring tasks; that's why you see fewer bank tellers and government clerks; AI is doing that work. What AI can do will get better and more interesting, but it's hard to say what human qualities it will be able to replicate. If your AI sits quietly with you while you talk through a problem, will it even know you're there?

AI is having a massive impact on the creative, knowledge, and manufacturing sectors, but companies in all sectors are using it, developing new ways to use it, or worrying about using it. AI is so powerful that its use is unavoidable. This much is well known. What is less well known is just how much AI will change our workplaces of the future. It's safe to say that the changes will be significant and ongoing, with some industries more impacted than others. And within each industry, you can find a wide range of opinions on what these impacts will be, and how many jobs AI will absorb or create.

As a worker, you need to stay nimble in the face of such significant uncertainty, being prepared to shift jobs or roles if you need to. But unless it's interesting to you, you shouldn't need to stay up to date on all the latest predictions; it could make you dizzy. You should be aware of and learn to use the AI in your industry. AI is a literacy and requires a certain kind of thinking. It's far from infallible, but AI tools are improving rapidly, since AI continuously learns and adapts, so we can assume they are here to stay. As is often said, 'AI won't replace you; a person using AI will.'

Automation and Your Job

While AI, specifically automation and digitalization, is significantly improving productivity and driving economic growth, the news for some jobs isn't good ... unless you are a robotics expert, of course. Robotics is the design, building and implementation of things that make manufacturing jobs obsolete, and it's a growing field. It requires specialized training, and the jobs tend to be geographically centralized.

Automation continues to cause a fall in manufacturing jobs, and that's unlikely to change. If you're considering moving into a manufacturing job, you should know that the jobs outlook isn't great, with employment falling to its lowest point since the 1940s. This is despite a boom in the construction of new facilities, driven by government spending, tax breaks, and other federal incentives. You're better off training in automation technology or the trades than hoping for the kind of steady manufacturing jobs that drove American prosperity in the 20th century. Ours is now a more service-based economy.

About 20% of North Americans are working in jobs that could be automated but aren't yet. Many of the positions requiring less skill are already gone like gas station attendants, bank tellers, and retail clerks.[iii] This makes career flexibility and adaptation necessary. White-collar jobs are not immune to these losses, though jobs requiring a high degree of social or emotional skill are less likely to be automated — because, in the end, people are still people. We form bonds, squabble, strive, and fall in love, just as we always have. Doing your job with a freshly broken heart will never get easier for you or for the person working next to you — unless the worker next to you is a robot. No amount of technology will change that or even smooth it out. So, your good thinking, creativity, and people skills will always be in demand. If these qualities aren't what you do best, you can improve them. How to do this is covered in the second half of the book.

Social Changes

We're experiencing significant social changes as well. Ours is an aging society with fewer children, older parents who are living longer, sometimes with chronic illnesses, and too often in social isolation. And more older adults are divorced, which means they're having to care for themselves. As the worldwide population continues to grow and age, older people are working longer with up to one in four still working at age sixty-five. This means some people stay in their jobs longer than expected, even though the labor market overall is getting younger as baby boomers age out of the workforce. Roughly one-third of the American labor force is made up of millennials (people born between 1981 and 1996), and a very large younger generation is quickly adding to those ranks every day.

> **FYI:** In 2024, 24% of men and about 16% of women aged sixty-five and older were still in the labor force.

As a large part of the workforce retires, new jobs are opening up, particularly in management positions. This might mean a new opportunity for you. It might mean you have a younger manager with a different style than what you're used to. What it also means is that there's an increased demand in certain fields, such as healthcare services and sustainability, so you may have more job opportunities in these sectors.

We're not just living longer. We're also becoming more educated. But before you start applying for more schooling, keep in mind that around half of the employed Canadian and U.S. labor forces have more knowledge and skill than they have the opportunity to apply in their current jobs. Unsurprisingly, overqualified workers are less satisfied in their jobs and more likely to look for new work. Although formal credentials are important, many employers still say their employees don't have the skills they need from formal education alone.

Moving internationally for work has become more common, whether through choice or climate-related displacement or for any other reason. This trend is changing North American labor markets, with more people coming and going. We work with people from more varied places, and migrants are younger and better educated than they used to be. You may find that the people you're working with have different needs or unfamiliar habits, and those differences can make your workforce stronger. Many of us are working with all kinds of people from all different places, so we're benefiting from their varied perspectives, and we have the opportunity to learn not only about a new culture, but about new ways of doing things. With open minds and hearts, we can benefit from this knowledge as we share our own. Sometimes we've got room to learn how to do this better.

Deo was born and raised in Burundi. After many years of school in Belgium, he earned a PhD in linguistics and moved several times before landing in Vancouver, where he plans to stay for good. Along the way, he and his wife had three kids, and he was sometimes separated from them for long periods, but Deo stayed focused on his dream, he persisted, and he got there. He was hired to teach full-time at the University of British Columbia, and he's finally doing the work he's so well suited for and that he loves. His experience, his mannerisms, his background, his culture, and his personality are all quite different from the people he works with. This is a big part of why they hired him. He brings the team something new. He makes the team stronger, and he's relatable to a whole host of students who might be feeling different and alone. But for Deo to be successful and to feel comfortable enough to stay long-term, his co-workers needed to be patient while he learned a new set of systems. They needed to have his back if others weren't so accommodating and to expand their work culture so that he could fit as well as they do.

Increasingly, we understand that diversity means that *we* change so that everyone fits, not that we've hired someone who is just like us with the exception of a single diversity criterion. Change can be slow and difficult, but companies with the most gender and ethnic diversity in their executive offices are most likely to have above average profitability. This benefit is as much as 33% more for ethnic diversity and a bit less for gender diversity. Knowing these truths makes it easier to address them by learning, mentoring, and willingly sharing knowledge, power, and influence with people who are too often denied it.

Economic and Geopolitical Patterns

There's no doubt we live in interesting times — though maybe not the best of times — with political and economic instability across the globe. The global COVID-19 pandemic amplified and exaggerated trends that were already happening. These changes mean you're working or looking for work in an unstable global environment, and it can also mean sudden, unexpected changes in your industry, the country, and the world overall. The stronger you are in your Career Imagination, the more likely you'll be able to adapt and make job changes according to what you want rather than by necessity.

When I talked to Laurel, she was experiencing upheaval in her government position and knew a career change was coming whether she wanted it or not. She was considering her options. She's had a varied career in both the public and private sectors, a lot of it in disaster relief. She's thinking of upskilling with a certificate in emergency management or possibly as a therapist specializing in disaster psychology. Laura also wants to do stand-up comedy to "fulfill the creator in me." Along the way she's learned more about her own process of job searching. She says, "It's interesting how one thing leads to another, and you can get pulled away from something unexpectedly. I should have talked to more people before I went into my job a few years ago. I might have made a different choice. So much is unexpected. Being flexible is helpful. I need to know the landscape so if I have to look for work again, I know where it is."

We know that increased global trade and better technology have made the world more connected and interdependent, resulting in significant economic and social changes. You may have already seen that more North American employers are using offshore workforces in places like India, Malaysia, and Brazil. This creates greater vulnerability and insecurity in our labor market since jobs can more easily be outsourced to places with cheap and abundant labor with lower wages — and fewer, if any, labor protections.

Global supply chains are intricately connected with carefully planned timelines marked by just-in-time manufacturing and lean inventory strategies that can be easily disrupted by delays or stoppages.

Wars and international conflicts, regardless of how far away they are, can impact these delicate systems, interrupting trade patterns and disrupting supply chains and production, transportation, and logistics channels. Port blockades and border closures further impede the movement of materials and products. The war in Ukraine, for instance, led to a rise in global food prices and price increases in oil and gas. Wars also displace people and damage infrastructure.

All of this can affect our jobs. You might have to tell the person at your sales counter that the order they placed three months ago is still not available. You might still be waiting for the fridge you bought and paid for, you can't remember when.

Global economic growth has remained strong by historic standards despite global instability and the economic difficulties ordinary people are facing. The prices we pay for the things we need are still high. Add to this the high cost of housing and child and elder care, as well as high student debt and medical expenses, and you see that the economic pain for the average person is real. These facts make it very maddening when leaders want to tell you that economically it's all good; they're just looking at the big picture, not the people picture.

Changes in the global market affect your job search efforts and make careful planning more important in career changes. In hard economic times, employers often slow hiring, which can make finding and shifting jobs more difficult. This makes it a good idea to know where you could move next and then develop a plan so you can do it on your own terms. While job rates are still pretty good, with unemployment still well below double digits, the long-term employment picture looks less certain. But let's remember, you'll always find a way to work, even if it looks different from previous generations. We're already seeing more self-employment, bartering, and people holding multiple jobs. Even though it's expected that we'll lose some bargaining power with employers in the near future, and it will likely become harder to switch jobs, the good news is there's a lot you can do to future-proof your career. The first step is having some understanding of the forces that affect the labor market so that you're looking in the right places with the right skills.

How Climate Change Affects Your Workplace

Alternative energy and sustainability are two of the biggest sources of new jobs overall and are fields you can move into if you're looking for a growth area. That's good news.

Climate change has a real effect on jobs and working people. Extreme weather events like floods, droughts, wildfires, and hurricanes can devastate communities, leading to health issues and often causing damage to businesses, infrastructure, transportation, industries, and agriculture. The damage can cause immediate job losses, but the clean-up and rebuilding can result in significant job gains.

Even when there isn't an acute event, we lose work hours when it's too hot. Extreme temperatures may not affect those in heat-controlled offices, but if you're in the trades, work as a first responder, or work in a hot building, you could be suffering greatly. And that makes it much harder to do your best work. High temperatures can also make us sick, and in some cases, can even be fatal. In 2020, Vancouver, which typically has a moderate climate, experienced an extended period of high heat that caused 619 unexpected deaths in three days.

The development of clean energy technology and transportation that helps reduce and address climate damage also leads to technological changes, more hiring in some areas, and new jobs in others. In 2022 worldwide, renewable energy and biofuels provided nearly 14 million jobs in manufacturing, installation, and operation. Clean and efficient power and transportation have direct job benefits, especially in rural areas where new technologies can be used to develop economic opportunities other than farming and often for better pay.

The World Economic Forum expects new jobs based on sustainable energy and climate mitigation will replace jobs lost to climate destruction, probably resulting in net job gains. And the World Bank says that climate action and mitigation and adaptation strategies will have "overwhelmingly positive jobs impacts." We love overwhelmingly positive jobs impacts! There will be much innovation. We'll learn to grow different crops and build more resilient buildings and infrastructure. And there might be a job you could love that you hadn't thought of because it didn't exist ten years ago. There might be the perfect job for you.

Conclusion

By now you should have something of an understanding of the greater forces affecting the labor market. These trends might seem high level and distant, but they already affect your workplace, career prospects, and the skills you need to succeed. You can use this information to make informed decisions about where the jobs of the future are likely to be, and where you can position yourself for the most success. You'll also be better equipped to notice shifts in your industry and know when it's time to adapt. Take your time to assess changes — no need to panic. Even radical changes usually unfold gradually, taking time to reach you and your job.

If you're in an industry that feels vulnerable, staying aware and agile will help you stay ahead and reduce your risk. If you've ever felt like your skills were being wasted at work, you're not alone. Research shows that many workers are overqualified for their current roles, which can be frustrating. While it's clear that the world of work is evolving, there will always be new opportunities, and with a big dream and the right strategy, you can find those jobs and thrive in them. In the following chapters, you'll learn how to make a plan that will help you reduce risk and adapt so you can have the career you most want to have. Everyone deserves decent work — and enough of it.

Take Action

Do the following exercises and make notes in your Career Imagination Journal:

1. Exercise your Career Imagination and dream about your blue-sky workday, then dream about your dream job. Ask yourself, what would make me feel like I'm doing the work I should be doing? What does my ideal work life feel like?

2. Learn about mega-trends so that you can drive your career in a direction where there are likely to be more rather than fewer

jobs. Don't panic, changes aren't happening as fast as some people fear.

3. Look for up-to-date information on the future of your industry. Here are some places to start:

    o   Government statistics publications such as StatsCan and the U.S. Bureau of Labor Statistics will show you current and past trends. An internet search including *"the relevant government agency"* (e.g., transportation, industry) and *"your industry"* will present you with easy-to-read short reports and graphs.

    o   Industry associations provide up-to-date information on trends and new advancements. Conference programs will show what industry leaders see as pressing concerns and opportunities for growth.

    o   A survey of job postings will help you identify current trends and skills gaps.

    o   An internet search of your industry and "job outlook" should provide you with predictions and statistics including a breakdown of which geographic regions have the greatest need. Look for reputable sources with enough funding to do in-depth research and fact-checking. E.g., *Forbes, McKinsey, Pew.*

Chapter Two

WAYS TO WORK: *Let Me Count the Ways*

The world is changing. Technology is reshaping jobs, workplaces, and career paths. And *how* we work is also changing. For one thing, we like staying home, with 12% of us working from home full-time and many more working in a hybrid model. Lots of us are doing gig work, often on the side and often unhappily. Self-employment is on the rise, which is good news for the dreamers who have plans to put their ideas into reality. The newly self-employed include contractors and consultants who might have been full-time employees in the past, and are still doing similar work, but at arm's length from their employer. Similarly, part-time work and non-permanent work are also increasing. Many of these changes improve work–life balance — and with advances in technology, more people can work in different ways.

If you like independence and flexibility, this should be good news for you, but it comes with some built-in stress. Some ways of working are less secure than others. For anyone looking to switch into a new career, understanding new employment patterns is valuable because it can help you take advantage of new opportunities — giving you more control over when you work, where you work, and how you work.

In the 21st century, we have an increased sense of insecurity and vulnerability about our jobs and careers. The worry is real. It's not just that many of us are now working for ourselves in one way or another, which brings with it considerable risk. There's greater instability in government and both small and large businesses. Where we once trusted that our large employer would continue indefinitely, we now understand that the business we work in could sell, move, shut down or lay off employees, as businesses are now more likely to prioritize short-term profits over long-term stability. We've seen large layoffs in government, not just in the United States. But we're not alone; we always have each other. This is what social networks are for (more on that later — it's really important). And when we build in career resilience, adaptability, and proactive planning, we can build stability for ourselves, even in uncertain times. The first step to being prepared is understanding current work trends.

On average, we're likely to stay in a job for about four years, a little less if we're women. Some of us don't like change, and if that's you, you might stay somewhere for a really long time. Whether through choice or necessity, workers are switching jobs at close to the same rate as they have for the last fifty years, but it's becoming easier to make that switch. We're more likely to leave a job by choice than because we've been laid off or fired, and at any given time, about half of us say we're thinking of quitting in the next year. "Adult gap year" is trending. If you want to change your job, you can, and statistically, you're likely to be happier in the new job after the first year.

In the coming years, we're likely to see ease of movement reduce a little because, as the labor market tightens, people will get cautious and stay in their jobs longer, resulting in fewer job openings. If people don't leave their jobs, fewer openings will appear for others. This will make finding a new job a little harder, but overall, we're still switching jobs more and doing it more easily.

Career change penalties are less than they used to be, with less stigma or concern for job switching, or for extended periods taken off work. So, we can move if we want to, or take some time, without worrying about a gap in our resume. Doing this too often, though, could mean you'll have some explaining to do. More than half of those who leave jobs say that in the new job, they enjoy better pay, better opportunities for advancement, and better work–life balance — so at the current time anyway, switching jobs has its benefits. Unsurprisingly, younger people leave jobs more often than their older counterparts. We know that people often stay in jobs they'd like to leave to keep healthcare benefits, and that's an important constraint that sometimes means a lateral move is the best option.

When we change jobs, we're more likely to also change industries, or ensure more flexible working arrangements like a shorter commute or more work-from-home options. We're still leaving for all the usual reasons: we don't like our boss, we don't see good opportunities for advancement, or we feel the pay isn't what it should or could be. More recently, people are also leaving because of issues with company culture, morale and level of engagement, as well as a desire for more flexibility. Whether you change jobs because you need to or have to, good planning is going to increase the chances that you end up in a better place rather than just *another* place.

Working from Home

For many people, working from home had been a fringe benefit for only a few until the pandemic caused it to explode overnight. Now that the pandemic is officially over, 12% of all American workers still work from home all the time, with a further 28% working a hybrid model. Among those whose jobs

> **FYI:** At the height of the pandemic no more than 55% of us worked at home The rest kept going in to work, although rarely just as usual.

can be done at home, 35% do it full time, five times the rate before the pandemic. A hybrid schedule is on the rise as workers assert their preferences and employers become more comfortable with the model. Some businesses are now even following a work from anywhere (WFA) model where employees are rarely, if ever, in the office. However, for some jobs, such as those that require high levels of internet security, there are fewer opportunities to work from home.

On the other hand, some businesses have rigidly demanded that employees return to the office, putting them in direct conflict with many of their workers. Apple CEO Tim Cook cited "the irreplaceable benefits of in-person collaboration" when ordering his employees to return to the office three non-consecutive days a week. His workers responded: "Office-bound work is a technology from the last century [...] It will make Apple younger, whiter, more male-dominated, more neuro-normative, more able-bodied; in short, it will lead to privileges deciding who can work for Apple, not who'd be the best fit."[iv] To date, the Apple employees have lost this battle. Unsurprisingly, Apple has made no comment on attrition of talent as a result, so we don't know if people are leaving as a result.

Working from home is directly tied to worker satisfaction. It's great if you can get it, but there's also a downside. There are mental health and personal well-being concerns for workers at home due to social isolation, as well as the difficulty for some to find an appropriate space to work in at home. And there remains a feeling that working from home can limit career advancement — "out of sight, out of mind," and while we can expect this to change over time, it might never go away entirely. Work is, after all, a social activity for most of us. It's harder to like and support people you don't know whose habits, weirdness, and triumphs are hidden from you. And employers worry that communication, collaboration, and culture are weakened when employees aren't in the office. If they want to keep this benefit, employees will need to find ways to prove them wrong, if possible.

There are plenty of work-from-home jobs available, and you can negotiate for it, even if it means you have to make a lateral move to a similar job. The time and cost savings can be enormous and may even be worth taking a slight pay cut. But keep an eye on the trends. If employment rates drop very much, workers lose bargaining power, and employers might demand more in-person work. Also, not all employers are confident that good work is being done from home, even though there's no good data showing that productivity drops at home. While it drops for some, it does not for most. In fact, there is data showing that on average, people do slightly more and sometimes better work when they work from home than when they work at the office. But a lot of employers don't *feel* this is true. Maybe the reason is a little sinister, in that ultimately, they don't trust their employees, even though there's a lot of benefit to employers when their employees work from home. People are likely to be more productive and motivated. More people will be interested in working for them, and they'll see lower absenteeism and turnover and obviously lower operating costs — people are paying for the office space themselves. However, many employers still have mixed feelings about it. Watch this space; the jury is out, but it's hard to imagine we won't see work from home increase in the future. It works, and people like it.

Managing Work-Life Balance

We hear a lot about gig work. This can include jobs like musician or contractor, but usually, we're referring to short-term flexible jobs using technology (apps) that make a far-off unseen or unavailable employer more possible. They range from freelance creative work to food delivery and car hire services that require few skills. They don't have benefits such

> **FYI:** Gig workers are sometimes called the "precariat," referring to the precarious nature of their work. The term was coined by Guy Standing in 2008.[iv]

as paid sick days, extended health coverage, pensions, or holiday pay,[v] and labor protections might also be limited, even very limited, depending on where you are. Gig work can provide a good supplemental income, so people often do this work on the side or in between better work opportunities, but it doesn't come with much security.

I spoke with Santiago, a stand-up comic in Denver who has a regular gig as a host at a local nightclub. It pays pretty well but doesn't provide enough work. He's a single dad, and the most important thing for him is flexibility, so he supplements his income by working in food delivery during the day, letting him be there for his kids before and after school. He gets a babysitter when he's out at night. This arrangement allows him to develop his performing career and properly care for his kids. When the kids are at school, and he's not delivering food, he can write and prepare for his work at night. It makes for long busy days, but he's career building. Eventually, he might be able to get more work in comedy or move into writing or do more hosting roles.

Part-time work (less than thirty hours per week) is another option. It often works well for stay-at-home parents, the semi-retired and students. But the part-time wage penalty is real. You'll probably earn nearly 30% less per hour than similar full-time workers, with the same rate of penalty regardless of race or gender.

Some people job-share, a relatively unusual part-time working arrangement where two employees share one full-time job. It can take quite a bit of coordination, and a lot can go wrong, but it can provide workers with flexibility while still doing meaningful work, although many employers don't like the arrangement. They have to pay double the benefits, and there are added administrative burdens for them. Finally, while the hours and extra freedom are appealing, part-timers generally receive fewer benefits (like healthcare and pensions), less mentoring, and fewer opportunities for growth. Companies are less likely to invest in you when they think you haven't made a serious investment in them, which working part-time sometimes signals. Most people don't usually stay in part-time work, but it can be useful for some.

Side Hustles & Multiple Jobs

Others look to add to their income by taking on an additional job. Multiple job holding is an interesting phenomenon because it seems to be difficult to measure, especially in the United States, where statistics are collected by states, not nationally, and because a lot of people work for cash on the side, and this doesn't get measured.

Most people with more than one job have a side hustle, meaning they have a dominant, regular job and then some work on the side.

Gig work, in particular, lends itself to side hustles, and so does consulting. A small business or microbusiness is another common side hustle. This might be furniture refinishing, importing, or selling at craft fairs or through online sites like Etsy and eBay. Many people work for cash cleaning houses, fixing appliances, babysitting, or providing eldercare. The side hustle sometimes becomes the supplementary income in early retirement, adding to pensions and government benefits. For those who do the same or similar work in the side hustle as they do in their main job, they need to watch for conflicts of interest and be prepared to declare the additional work. Regardless of the method, more people at all income levels are holding more than one job. Some of these people are really struggling, but for the hustlers, holding more than one job can work out great. They work multiple jobs to make more money and seize more opportunities.

Some experts, including me, predict that the trend of people holding multiple jobs will increase significantly as technology changes the nature of work and if the cost of living remains high. If you're a dreamer with thoughts of owning your own small business one day, maybe turning that hobby into a revenue generator, this is how it might happen: a little on the side until you can grow it enough to support yourself full-time and maybe even hire some people to help.

I interviewed Carl, a tech worker in Atlanta with over twenty years of experience who has more than one job. He also has a side hustle as a co-owner of a courier company with ten large vans shipping specialty goods across the south and up as far as New York City. He has three cell phones, so he can keep everything separate and manages his part of the business mostly from his phones. He insists it only takes a few minutes a day, which frees him up to "have a full-time job on the side." The key to his success is a good partner who works full time in the business. Carl also has the experience to properly understand his business and the organizational ability to keep things in order.

Non-Permanent Work

At the same time as workers are demanding greater flexibility and autonomy, including the option to work from home, some employers are giving it to them in the form of non-permanent work. This refers to jobs that are not long term (usually lasting no more than two years) that don't offer the job security of permanent employment. Most industries have at least some segments of workers on non-permanent contracts, including government, education, healthcare, technology, and the creative industries. These are a bit more stable than gig work, but there is still a high degree of insecurity associated with the full-time position coming to an inevitable end when the contract expires. Non-permanence works well for people with specialist skills who are in high demand and can charge a premium, working on their own terms. But for many of us, temporary work comes with real problems, namely a lack of healthcare benefits, pensions, job security, and worker rights. Add to this the lack of community, mentorship, and training that usually goes with a permanent job.

As with part-time work, employers like temporary work because it offers them greater flexibility and represents significant cost-savings. It can offer you greater flexibility too; good news if that's what you want, and many of us do. Learning new skills and staying flexible can help you navigate this uncertainty and make you more employable.

And there are times in a life and a career when non-permanence works well, perhaps when caring for family or later in a career. It can be a good way to extend a career and delay retirement. People in early and mid-career will often work non-permanent as a stopgap until something more solid comes along. Others figure it out, get good at getting the next gig, and it starts to work really well. To do it long term, they need to maintain their social connections and keep up their professional development on their own.

Things may be a little more challenging if you're a non-permanent worker in a large technology firm. These companies often use staffing agencies to hire huge non-permanent workforces of skilled workers, mostly young and often underpaid, without status or benefits, and sometimes forming the majority of their workforce. Employers like it because it costs them less in the long run and it offers a lot of flexibility. They don't need to make a commitment, and regardless of what they promise, many have a policy not to move someone from non-permanent to permanent.

These very large tech companies have a lot of status and can pay very well, but they sometimes have difficult cultures and things they don't want people to talk about. They often require employees to sign non-disclosure agreements, to prevent them from discussing the conditions of their employment. Being able to share information about employers, your rights, pay, and benefits is an important function of our social networks. It keeps us safe, helps us get a fair wage, and, importantly, helps us avoid bad bosses. Our research shows that for many people, large tech companies are a great way to gain experience and build a resume, but there might be better options for long-term employment, work–life balance, and liking your manager. And the days of lucrative contracts for early career professionals in big tech seem to be pretty much over.

Contracting

Contract work is a form of non-permanent work where you're hired for a specific short-term job, such as for a particular project or to cover another worker's leave of absence. These contracts can offer the best and the worst of both worlds. Contract workers enjoy a lot of autonomy, choosing when they want to work and the type of work — often getting a variety of experience and the opportunity to meet many people in their industry. This can help you develop skills and network for future work. And contractors are often paid a higher rate. This can be very good work, especially for those who are more highly educated and skilled, providing autonomy, flexibility, and greater control over their lives.

On the other hand, you can expect to be looking for new work when the contract ends. And, as with any non-permanent work, there are few, if any, benefits, no pension, no paid sick days, and limited on-the-job training. It can really hurt your professional growth if you don't have a mentor or sponsor to help you improve your skills and advance. If you're in this position, you'll need to plan for growth on your own. And of course, you don't make money when you're out of work and looking for your next contract.

If you're thinking about using contract work as a stepping stone towards a career change or you just want to try something new, it's good to know that you're most likely to do well if you have a specialty or can fill a niche. Otherwise, it can be hard to find that next contract.

How Do Contract Workers Succeed?

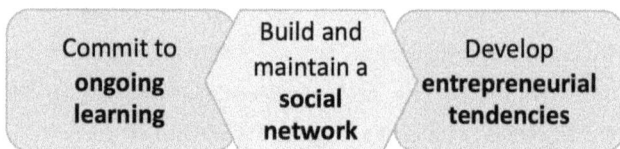

Commit to ongoing learning	Build and maintain a social network	Develop entrepreneurial tendencies

Contract workers need strong internal motivation to achieve success, to enjoy, or at least tolerate, some risk, and possess a willingness to learn new patterns and skills with each new contract. They also need to be able to engage socially to get noticed and be more likely to get supported or promoted. If you're a contract worker, this has to happen in the relatively short time you're in the job. Finally, you need to be curious, to continue looking for new work even while you're already working, and to believe that you'll get the next contract and that it will be better than the last.

If contracting is for you, you can develop and foster all these traits. For sure, an introvert isn't going to learn to become an extrovert, but they can learn to build a high-functioning social network, even if it's small. And we can find ways to keep learning that we can love; it doesn't have to mean sitting in a classroom. You'll find more on these topics in Chapters Eight and Nine.

FYI: People who have the most success working as contractors, consultants, and otherwise independently usually have three interconnected qualities: 1) a commitment to continuous learning; 2) a strong social network; and 3) the entrepreneurial traits of *ambition, sociability, optimism, and curiosity.*

Being Your Own Boss

Did you know that the self-employed are likely to be happier and express a higher sense of well-being? This is despite the fact that, on average, you'll make less money, work more hours, and won't have a pension, paid sick time, or health benefits. It's also harder to get a loan, even though you'll need money to make that creative vision a reality. But you'll be able to set your own schedule and choose your customers and projects, so you'll have a lot of control and freedom. If this is appealing and you're willing to accept the downsides, then you may just have the personality necessary to be a successful business owner!

The key personality traits necessary for successful self-employment and entrepreneurship are optimism, confidence, and ambition; the rest follow from these. It helps if you have emotional stability, are open to new experiences, and tend to be a social person. You need a high tolerance for risk, the ability to keep going in the face of uncertainty, and a general optimism.

How Do Entrepreneurs Succeed?

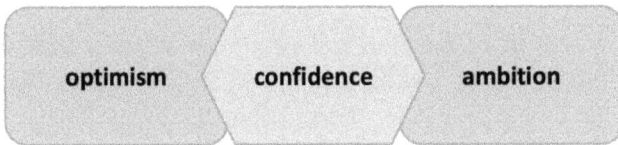

optimism   confidence   ambition

With the right mindset, you will proceed, tackling the challenges as they come, focusing on problem-solving rather than how the difficulty makes you feel. The more successful entrepreneurs have a lot of curiosity, a drive to learn more, and a desire to achieve more. If you're more Eeyore than Winnie-the-Pooh, self-employment might be harder for you. But if you have an existing client base or a market that is familiar with you and what you're selling, then the risk is much lower, and it may be a good decision for you.

Pros and Cons of Self-Employment

Pros	Cons
You are likely to be happier and feel an overall higher sense of well-being.	Overall, the self-employed earn less and have fewer, if any, benefits such as pension and sick pay. (However, if you have a specialty skill, you might earn more.)
You gain flexibility and independence.	You alone must absorb the risk and volatility.
You can have creative and operational control.	You may lack the resources necessary to realize your vision for your business.
If the business does well, you do well.	Income can be volatile and insecure.

There are many types of self-employment jobs, and if you're serious about being your own boss, you've got a number of options.

Consultants, freelancers, and independent professionals are experts hired to provide advice in a particular field. Before becoming a consultant, you'll need to make sure you have some clients lined up, which is why it's usually done later when you've got a reputation and a network of contacts.

Savana is a sign language interpreter, something she never thought of as a profession. She learned American Sign Language (ASL) in high school because she was interested in it, then went on to get an associate degree in speech pathology. She works with six different agencies that place her as frequently as she likes, often in courtrooms. As a freelancer, she needs to purchase her own medical insurance and will have to plan for her own pension, but she's independent and working in a field that she loves where she can make a positive difference with people who really need her skills.

She's a social person, which is a good indicator of her future success, but she has to be silent in the courtroom, and it can get lonely.

If you're thinking of starting a business, you have some more choices. You might own the business on your own or with a partner. If you have a partner, make sure you have a partnership agreement that outlines roles and responsibilities, and, crucially, provides an exit plan if someone wants to leave or sell, or if they pass away. It's best not to assume it's everlasting love; you never know what course life will take. You may choose to be incorporated — it usually depends on sales volume since incorporation has some costs attached to it, but it's important if you have any concerns about liability. On the flip side, micropreneurs have no employees. These are professionals or crafters and hobbyists who've turned their passion into a business, albeit a small one. Others sell a small range of products they've either produced themselves or purchased from someone else to resell. The running shoe resale market, for instance, can be big business and the barriers to entry are low.

Cheyanne is a hairstylist who has owned a successful salon in a small city for many years. In the salon, she sells a wide range of carefully considered, premium hair care products that are sold to her by various distributors who take a cut of each sale. Cheyanne was thinking about a change but wasn't ready to fully leave working life. Her solution was to buy the exclusive North American rights to sell a line of popular hair care products from Germany. With the help of a salesperson, Cheyanne now distributes these products to other salons for a markup, expanding her business and helping her bridge into retirement. She set this up as a separate business from the salon, so there's no overlap when she sells the shop.

Paul worked for ten years in accounting for a large paint manufacturing company. There was a lot of pressure, "particularly at quarter end, that's four times a year — that was really stressful." He left to start a soap company. He says he'll never take another job, "I'm so relaxed." He sells in markets, on the street, and online. His company provides him with the opportunity to be creative, make some money, and be independent.

Whatever your business, before starting it, you'll have to consider a few things. Market entry barriers or the cost to start up come first. You'll look at the amount of competition in your area, and then maybe broaden your geographic reach, this includes your marketing, even if you're selling online. It'll help if you do some research on how much your industry is changing due to innovation and technology. And it'll help some more if you do some research on the potential for growth in your business.

Try this: *Research is a good thing to do while you're in the dreaming or Career Imagination stage. It helps you plan and keeps you motivated while you move closer to your goal. Start your research small by confirming an unproven assumption you find you have.*

Owning our own business is an important part of our collective dream, and the benefits are very appealing. At least two-thirds of all North Americans would like to run their own business one day. The reasons are obvious: independence, creativity, and realizing the benefits of your own labor. There is also often a higher status attached to being a job creator and independent businessperson. If you're one of the dreamers, you've probably already envisioned the flexibility, independence and creative and operational control you could achieve with your own business.

If you want to buy into an existing brand, think about running a franchise. In a franchise, you'll generally pay a percentage of your revenue to the parent company in exchange for the established product and brand, ongoing marketing, knowledge sharing, and operational processes. You'll have to meet their standards, be subject to oversight, and follow specific rules. But because the brand is established, the risk will be much lower than starting something similar on your own or buying an existing independent business.

There are lots of organizations that can help you figure out what the best franchise opportunity is for you. Be sure to talk to plenty of people who have taken that route before you make a commitment and consider the market you will operate in. You'll need to know how strong the brand is there and how much competition you will have. A good franchise brand will help you with these things, but they'll want to see that you've done some market research first and that you've got enough money to get started.

Semi-Retirement

Many people need to, and sometimes want to, keep working for a while after they retire from their careers. There are a lot of things you can do, but most successful workers choose something they're good at, or can become good at fairly quickly. Think about how hard you want to work, if you're willing to upskill, and how much stress you're willing to tolerate. Many small businesses are willing to hire older people, and your maturity and reliability is a benefit to them, one they are willing to pay a premium for, but you'll likely have to ask for that raise.

Take this quiz to focus your semi-retirement plans			
Answer yes (Y) or no (N).		Y	N
1	Do you want to work for yourself?		
2	Do you want to work for someone else?		
3	Are you willing to invest money in a new venture?		
4	Are you willing to invest time in a new venture?		
Answer high (H), medium (M), or low (L).	H	M	L
5	How much stress are you willing to tolerate?		
6	How willing are you to upskill or retrain?		
7	How many hours a week do you want to work?		
8	How long do you want to keep working?		
9	How much time off do you want?		
10	How much flexibility do you need?		
11	How physically able are you?		

You might build on something you already really enjoy doing and turn it into something people will pay for, maybe starting your own small business. The key here is to make sure there's good demand, like trades work, or something you're very skilled at, like furniture building. Consider how much retraining you'll need as well as how long it will take you to get good at something new. Chapter Nine addresses upskilling in some detail.

Anne-Marie is a middle-school teacher. She's too young to retire completely but too old to keep doing what she's been doing for thirty years. She's a teacher because she loves learning, and it provides the opportunity for endless challenge and variety. Early in her career, she was motivated by knowing that she was making a difference, but now her goals for her students are much simpler, "I just want them to be healthy and not be a jerk, to be kind to one another." In the next few years, she'll have a full pension, which she'll supplement with some part-time work. With a bit of planning and maybe some new training, her part-time work will suit her age, experience, and interests, and she can continue doing it as long as she likes.

Stephen worked for many years as a care aid in a senior's home. The pandemic took its toll, and he left a little earlier than he had planned. He has a pension but it's not really enough to cover the cost-of-living increases. He supplemented his income with some house cleaning since then and before he retired, but with inflation, he needs to do more. Now he's added some private eldercare for people he's known for a long time. He checks in on them, does some grocery shopping, and in some cases reports back to family who live far away. Both jobs allow him to draw on his strengths of being personable and caring, and neither causes too much stress since he doesn't have to work for anyone he doesn't want to. Importantly, he gets to keep doing the caring work that is so fulfilling, and he can afford to spend a month every year in Australia.

Jobs Suitable for Semi-retirement	
Lower skilled / lower stress	**Higher skilled / higher reward**
<ul><li>Wine tasting host</li><li>Driving</li><li>Babysitting</li><li>Blade sharpening</li><li>Car detailing</li><li>Dog walking</li><li>Vending machine ownership / management</li><li>Furniture refinishing</li><li>House cleaning</li><li>Tourism ambassador</li></ul>	<ul><li>All the trades</li><li>Vocational teaching</li><li>Small appliance repair</li><li>Real estate services</li><li>Small business management</li><li>Eldercare</li><li>Landscaping</li><li>Specialty food and drink making</li><li>Collectibles buy and sell</li><li>Landscaping / hardscaping</li><li>Light / heavy equipment operator</li><li>Training of large temporary workforces</li><li>Furniture repair</li><li>Teaching specialty skills</li><li>App development</li><li>Freelancing</li><li>Virtual assistant</li></ul>
Artistic Endeavors <ul><li>Mural painting</li><li>Selling arts and crafts in markets and online marketplaces</li><li>Furniture making</li><li>Creating YouTube videos</li><li>Photography</li></ul>	

Accessibility

It's getting easier for people with disabilities to work in an average workplace, but it's still hard. Technology can be helpful, often life-changing, and so is human rights legislation that requires employers to make reasonable accommodations, or accommodations that don't pass the point of "undue hardship." Invisible disabilities, including neurodiversity, neurodegenerative disorders such as multiple sclerosis, chronic pain, and chronic fatigue, are sometimes not recognized or understood very well, so workers facing these challenges may have a harder time getting needed supports in the workplace.

If you have a disability, look for openness to difference, empathy, and approachability in your employer and managers. Accommodation can include greater opportunities to work from home, allowance for microbreaks, choices in communication methods, or modified work hours. Some people choose to disclose a disability in the hiring process, some wait until they are hired, and some never do. Disclosure is up to the individual.

Leah is an accessibility specialist helping a large organization meet the needs of its staff with disabilities. As someone with hearing loss, for the first time in her adult career, she feels supported in her work by a manager who is approachable, empathetic, and understands her needs and those of the people she assists. She encourages people to ask potential employers what accommodation they offer, so as workers they have what they need to do the job. She says, "Nothing asked, nothing said, nothing gets done." By asking for accommodation, you're more likely to end up with a job that can mold to you, rather than you molding to the job, because, after all, the person with the disability is the expert on what works for them.

Leah offers some more good advice that is backed up by our research, "Don't be afraid to ask what accommodations they (a potential employer) offer. Don't be afraid to wait to disclose. Culturally, sometimes people don't want to be different, so they don't want to disclose. This could also be due to trauma from past jobs. But ask yourself, what do you need to do to be able to do this job? If you get what you need, you don't mold to the job, the job molds to you." And for employers, she asks, "How willing are you to hire someone with a disability? The person with a disability is the expert and what works for them. You need to be open so you can figure it out together." This way employers can hire top talent that will be motivated and loyal.

Working in a Labor Union

Some people work in a union shop, but membership is in decline, particularly in the United States. In the United States and Canada, membership is usually mandatory; in the United Kingdom, you can often opt out. Labor unions work on collective action, and it's the only way they work. While an employer can lay off, fire, or otherwise constrain one or a few employees, it's much harder to take such action against an entire workforce. Most of the benefits workers gained in the 20th century, such as weekends, holidays, safety measures, and overtime pay, were achieved through the collective action of labor unions. Today, unions are helping workers with modern benefits like fair pay for screenwriters whose productions are seen on streaming services and work-from-home allowances.

> **FYI:** 10% of Americans belong to a labor union, about half of what it was in 1990. One third of Canadians are union members. Two thirds of Americans believe unions are generally good for workers. (Pew Research)

Unionized workers generally get paid more than their non-union counterparts. However, being in a union is not for everyone. Unions have a lot of rules and there are consequences for breaking them. And sometimes they protect bad employees, but they also protect good ones.

Try this: Learn about your potential employer's benefits, such as health coverage and time off — some companies offer much more than others. Mandatory paid leave and holidays vary from country to country.

Conclusion

When it comes to choosing how you work today, many are spoiled for choice. If you think there's a better way for you to work, then you should consider your options. As your career progresses, more options become available to you, and you can make a shift in one or more new directions if you want to.

In the future of work, more of us will be working part-time, on a non-permanent basis, or for ourselves. If we are well prepared, we'll be ready for the risks this brings, and then we can enjoy the benefits of greater fulfillment, autonomy, flexibility, and quite possibly more money. Consider your personality and if you have what it takes to assume more risk to get more reward. Then, take the time to put the pieces in place so you can be successful sooner rather than later. This includes exercising your Career Imagination so that what comes next is as fulfilling as possible.

Take Action

Do the following exercises and make notes in your Career Imagination Journal:

1. Consider how you like to work. Write down some jobs that already work like that.

2. Determine if you have the right skills, experience, and personality traits for the kind of work you want. If you don't, see what you can do to develop what you need. The second half of this book addresses how to do this in practical terms.

Chapter Three

THE FUTURE OF JOBS: *Where Do I Fit, Where Can I Go?*

Before you take the risk and the effort to start a new career, you want to make sure you're getting yourself into something you'll enjoy, but also that the new job will still be there in five years or more. Below is an overview of what is expected for the future of work in several broad categories of jobs. There are heaps of careers that fall outside these buckets and many that fall into multiple buckets. The findings are generally unsurprising, but on offer are some details to help with your planning.

Knowledge Workers

Knowledge workers are professionals with specialized knowledge whose main value is in what they know and how they apply it. They work in roles such as human resources (HR), marketing, accounting, planning, and many other office jobs. Their work generally has some level of complexity and is unlikely to conform to a particular set of rules or routines. They use critical and creative thinking to solve problems and advance mandates. This isn't to say that people in other fields — trades, for instance — aren't also using a great deal of knowledge and complex thinking, but this term is used to capture those whose primary asset at work is information and its organization.

Jobs for knowledge workers are changing considerably, moving from largely full-time, permanent work to contract and non-permanent positions. Working from home is on the rise, but perhaps less than expected. Technology, most notably increasing digitalization, AI, and data management, is also driving change for knowledge workers and creating a degree of insecurity, especially for those who haven't learned to use the new tools. Knowledge workers should be prepared for change by keeping their tech skills up to date and being ready to change jobs as the market they are in changes. They should also make sure they can demonstrate good people and leadership skills.

Education & Teaching

There's a steady demand for teachers and countless support jobs available in the system, ranging from operations workers, such as school janitors, to highly skilled tech workers and administrators. Some people consider teaching a particularly important profession for the impact it has on both individuals and society. Interacting with a willing learner is one of the most rewarding things in the world, as is seeing a troubled learner grow and move past obstacles. As a teacher, it's not usually difficult to see that you're making a difference.

While teacher shortages are widespread, there's a particular demand for vocational teachers, those who specialize in teaching specific trades or practical learning, often at colleges and usually part-time. Large numbers of baby boomers are retiring, accelerated by the pandemic, and the retention of public-school teachers in the first five years has always been a problem. There are real challenges for public school teachers that have led to serious teacher shortages globally. This is partly because teaching is a challenging profession that can take an emotional toll, and burnout happens all too often. Perhaps the two biggest challenges for teachers are the increased off-loading of social problems to schools and the constraints around what is allowed to be taught in the classroom.

In the United States, shortages are most acute in rural areas and low-income urban areas. In Canada, schools are funded centrally, public school teachers are unionized, and professional development is actively supported. Curriculums are also centrally developed, but teachers have a lot of freedom in how they cover content in their classrooms, with independence being carefully protected. However, teaching is becoming more challenging everywhere in the modern era. Teachers spend a lot of time dealing with noneducation issues, such as phone use and the distractions of social media. If you're okay with these challenges and feel you could make a difference, teaching might be a good choice for you.

Try this: Do your research and choose a job carefully, considering practices, culture, and regulations in the region you plan to work in. When you get tired, and you will, consider a shift to another kind of job, maybe still in education if it continues to be where your passion lies.

If working with children or teens is not appealing but you still want to teach, post-secondary teaching has some real benefits. It ranges from low-paid, non-permanent sessional or adjunct work to highly paid professorships that are rooted in research. In between are full-time, permanent teaching positions, such as lecturers, who aren't paid to research, just to teach. Academic freedom should allow for a high degree of independence in the classroom. Post-secondary students generally take the education they are paying for seriously, although they typically feel overworked and often don't do their readings! Post-secondary and academic teaching also come with all the benefits of teaching in the public system but without the most challenging pressures.

Finance & Banking

In general, finance and banking jobs are high status and often high paying, with plenty of room for advancement and relocation. The required skill set is expanding with ever-increasing online operations and vastly greater needs for security. The industry is changing, requiring new kinds of workers. Fintech, digital commerce, cybersecurity, and automation are the greatest growth areas, and in all these areas, there's a demand for specialized skills, like compliance, knowledge of data visualization tools, AI and machine learning, and database management systems.

But it's a high-pressure industry with the highest turnover rates of any profession. The jobs can be very demanding, with long hours and high stress; there's a lot of money on the line. Often, turnover is driven by the desire for advancement in a field where there are always a lot of opportunities. However, sometimes people leave the profession for something that fits better with their values or a desire for a better work–life balance. The old trope of the jaded banker retiring early to help save the children exists for a reason.

Government

Now is a difficult time for work with the federal government in both Canada and the United States, but if you're committed to having a government job, look at regional organizations, health authorities, parks, regulators, education, justice, and everything in between. Just because you've only ever worked in transportation doesn't mean there isn't a role for you in finance.

Government jobs are extremely varied. Some are unionized with all the security and benefits (and frustrations) that go with that, but many are now contract positions without permanence or benefits, although contract positions often pay well. Government pensions can be such a strong appeal that people starting to think about retirement may take a government job just for that. For the permanent workforce, government workers often benefit from the camaraderie and cooperation that comes with working in large, stable teams. More importantly, what is often underreported is the opportunity for challenge, impact, and service, stemming from the knowledge that workers are providing services essential to the running of their community and their country.

Other Professionals

Professionals like lawyers, accountants, and high-level managers are generally highly paid and there's usually strong demand, making it worth the investment if it's what you want to do. These jobs require significant levels of critical thinking and often administrative skills, as well as extensive education, certification, and ongoing professional development. The hours are often long, and your work–life balance can suffer. It's a trade-off that people in these fields have to make, unless and until they can become a consultant and work on their own terms.

STEM Jobs

There's a reason schools place so much emphasis on growing their science, technology, engineering, and math (STEM) programs. There's an evergreen demand for workers with knowledge in these fields. McKinsey estimates that the demand for health sector workers and other STEM-related professionals will grow by 17% to 30% between 2022 and 2030. While the World Economic Forum says, "the future of jobs is green," with the demand for sustainability specialists and green energy professionals continuing to grow. Generally, you need at least a bachelor's degree in the field you're looking in, but you can also take specialized courses to add to your existing knowledge.

I met Stefan at the American Chemical Society Conference. He has a PhD and a post-doctorate. Like many scientists, he has a very specific research question he's interested in continuing to investigate. He's aware of the corporate opportunities available to him, but he's more interested in staying in public research as long as the congressional grant he's been working on gets continued. For Stefan, the values of what he's working on matter. He's highly skilled, working in a field with a promising future, so there will be work for him and the money will follow.

At the same conference, I spoke to chemists Lucia and Simone. They both work in research and development at Apple, improving the user experience (UX). Specifically, they work on screens and displays. They were a little younger and a little more excited than most of the scientists I spoke to. The work is interesting and "the money is really good," they say. They got premium jobs based in large part on their grades and internships, and now they have some top-flight experience to add to their resumes if the time comes to move on to something new.

Tech Jobs

If you're interested in a job in the tech sector, there are still many opportunities with the overwhelming majority of tech managers reporting that they have difficulty hiring the talent they need. AI and machine learning specialists top the list of fast-growing jobs. As noted earlier, the greatest growths in tech jobs continue to be in fintech, cybersecurity, and e-commerce. Telehealth, online education platforms, business intelligence, big data, sustainability technology, and transit production are also growth areas.

The industry is now well-established, so getting a job, especially a first job, is not as easy as it was; the labor shortages that have marked this sector over the last thirty years have flattened out as people trained up and went where the jobs were. There's still a huge demand for tech labor, and a real shortage of people with the right skills. But we've probably come to the end of the high-paying early career job in big tech. It doesn't make sense to pay $150,000 or more for a low- to mid-level role when it can now be outsourced to people offshore and/or automated with AI. It means that many people will need to gain experience outside big tech before they can cross that gulley from entry-level to high-paying skilled and experienced tech professional. This is one of those industries where what you can do is much more important to potential employers than where you went to school.

Jay recently left his high-paying tech job to start his own tech firm. He told us, "I would not hire myself back in Silicon Valley anymore." Referring to his right-out-of-college, high-paying, high-status tech job, "I think we've reached the peak of that in my thoughts."

Despite huge layoffs in big tech, who over-hired at the start of the pandemic as the world moved online, there's still a tech talent gap in the economy overall. Healthcare, government, and education are all big tech users, and they tend to provide long-term stable jobs with labor protections and good benefits. The salaries are almost certainly not as high as in big tech, but the risk is much lower, and the work–life balance might be better.

> **FYI:** In 2025, more than 80% of executives reported that they do not have the technology talent they need to drive their digital transformation and that a lack of appropriate talent is holding back that transformation.

In the private sector, retail is a big user of tech, with everything from online shopping functions to human resource management software. Manufacturing uses tech in all the usual ways but also requires sophisticated optimization systems, data management, and trend analysis. An ongoing challenge for firms is hiring people with the right technology skills *and* the necessary soft skills — most specifically, people skills, collaboration, and creative thinking.

Try this: If you're thinking of a career that involves tech, build up your tech skills but work on the soft stuff also — employers are looking for workers who think creatively, are problem-solvers, and are good with people and teams.

Healthcare Jobs

Overall, the healthcare sector is hiring. It continues to face huge labor shortages, and this will continue for some time as the population ages, retirement levels rise, and the system continues to recover from the pandemic. But like anywhere, demand isn't even, with more need in some places than others.

Healthcare jobs often pay well, with support occupations, such as home health and personal care aides, medical transcriptionists, and occupational therapy assistants, paying slightly lower salaries. But people don't usually go into healthcare because of the money. Instead, the drive to help people is profound. And while there are many rewards when you work in this sector, working conditions, made worse by labor shortages, can be challenging. On a positive note, there are endless ways to work in healthcare, ranging from a regular Monday-to-Friday workweek to shift work, part-time, overtime, and everything in between. If the job you have isn't working, mobility (the ability to switch jobs) in the healthcare sector is good.

Alison is a physiotherapist who chose this work because it allows her to be in healthcare and satisfy her overwhelming drive to help, but it also allows her to have a life outside of work, which she very much does. She spends a lot of time hiking, skiing, and climbing in the backcountry near her rural home, and she volunteers with search and rescue where her professional skills are a real asset. The work, both paid and volunteer, is intellectually challenging, drawing on many important parts of her, including her creativity and compassion. She is learning on the job every day and helps people live better, safer, more comfortable lives. The opportunities for growth are significant, and she thinks about getting a PhD or opening her own clinic. Alison took a long time to reach this position of strength, including a two-year master's degree that was expensive and difficult, but here she is.

Pharmacies can be a good hybrid employer, allowing people to work in healthcare but also in the private or public sector, depending on their preference. Related roles include pharmacy technicians, assistants, managers, and clerks.

Personal care services are also in demand. Think health and wellness, eldercare, athletic training, dog walking, and anything else that provides a personal care service to people. The median annual wage is below the national average, but there's considerable flexibility and often a good work–life balance. You're sometimes able to choose your own hours, but often services have to be available where and when people can attend, and given the lower wages, many people in this sector work longer hours to maintain a sustainable living, turning out the lights in the studio long after everyone else has settled in at home.

There's significant opportunity to be self-employed in this sector, which comes with risk and may require different skills than the service skills you were trained in, but independence can be very attractive. If you have specialized skills that are in demand and a good brand, you can charge a premium. In all, this is often satisfying work where you can work with people, helping them live better lives, and doing something you love. However, the hard work of making a living never ends, and there are limited opportunities to advance.

Trades Jobs

Let's be clear; trades jobs are very often great jobs. They usually pay well, especially once you have some experience, own your own business, or work in a union. Average wages in this sector rose by more than 20% at the beginning of the pandemic, and for many, that level of growth has continued. There's always lots of work, and in many instances, it's future-proof: we'll always need plumbers, carpenters, and mechanics. And most of these jobs are hard to automate unless they can be done repeatedly exactly the same in an assembly-line fashion. But no one wants an automated landscaper.

It's estimated that for every five baby boomers retiring from the trades, there are only two younger people moving in to take their place. This is probably due to the undervaluation of blue-collar work and an overvaluation of four-year college degrees, but maybe by now, we've moved past this perception. Whatever the reason, a skilled worker shortage has a significant impact on our economy, affecting our ability to maintain and build infrastructure, including housing and national defense. So, if you go into the trades, you'll find an industry ready and waiting for you.

In the future of work, the tools you use might change, and some of the tasks might get automated, but the water will continue to flow, and someone will need to know how to manage it. A bonus is that there's often some really good camaraderie available in jobs that are physical and interdependent. Many people choose a trades job because they like physicality, rather than being tied to a desk and a screen. You also make money while others are in college, and you can work when you like because there's always more work.

The catch is that in order to make *good* money, you need to train and probably get ticketed, which means you've attained a certain level of expertise. If your goal is to work independently, you need to be able to certify the work you do, which is only legal if you're ticketed, and you might have to develop managerial skills so you can manage clients and learn to administer materials, time, and budget. Tradespeople can often interpret technical drawings and be excellent problem-solvers and troubleshooters; the same isn't always true for those with a four-year degree.

Try this: *If you want to work in the trades, think about how you can get certified. If you don't get ticketed, you won't be able to achieve higher levels of income and independence, and over time, the physical work can really take its toll on your body.*

Gabriel is an experienced construction worker who eventually made his way into management through a friend since working as a welder for someone else just didn't pay enough, and he felt his body was getting a little old anyway. "I feel like I'm cheating as a manager; it's so easy." He's learning management skills and learning to speak Spanish since so many of his workers don't speak English. Upskilling is giving him job security so he can keep feeling like he's cheating for a really long time if he wants to.

You don't need to be young to move into the trades. If you're an unhappy tech worker, think about what it would be like to work with pastry, machines, or plants all day. The skilled trades are many and varied … and they're hiring.

Like with any job, your first trades job might not be the one you want, but it's definitely out there, and you won't have to look too hard. The best way to start is to talk to people and let them know that you're looking for work and what you can do. At first, but not for too long, be prepared to do some low- or no-skill work that's below your level of training. If that doesn't change quickly enough, build relationships and ask around; there will be someone who needs what you have to offer, especially if you can deliver it with some professionalism and, even better, with some good humor.

Early on, you should expect some guidance, mentoring, and training beyond what you got in school. If that's not on offer and you need it, you'll do your job, take your check and keep looking for somewhere that is prepared to invest in you. You may need to look outside your region if your market is a little over-saturated. It's likely that jobs in your area will free up before too long, but if you want to work now, consider looking a little away from home if you need to.

Trades Jobs:

- arborists and landscapers
- carpenters
- construction laborers
- electricians
- cook and baker
- glaziers
- heating, air-conditioning, and refrigeration mechanics and installers
- industrial machinery mechanics, machinery maintenance workers, and millwrights
- ironworkers
- material-moving-machine operators
- plumbers, pipefitters, and steamfitters
- solar photovoltaic installers
- welders, cutters, solderers, and braziers
- wind turbine service technicians
- barbers and hair stylists

Source: McKinsey & Company

Daniel started his plumbing job in the dead of winter with no experience. The first day they were doing repairs in a chocolate factory, which seemed promising. The next week, he was asked to dig a ditch in the rain with no supervision. He was worried that he would puncture a line or go in the wrong direction, ruining the client's garden, and he was plenty unhappy with the stress this caused him. His boss figured out pretty quickly that he needed to offer Dan more guidance, and Dan, being a quick learner, had picked up a ton of skills by the time summer came around. Within a year, he was doing the work of a plumber, often unsupervised, and he knew this was the work for him.

Without his ticket, he's vulnerable to any changes in the company, and his wages will stay low. But now he has the information he needs, and getting formal training will give him security in the profession he loves. If he can overcome his anxiety around schooling, doing the schoolwork will be pretty easy, as he's already got many of the skills he needs and a place to apprentice. Alternatively, he can start his own business, probably mostly working on smaller jobs, and there will never be a shortage of work; but he'll always need a ticketed professional to approve his work.

The skilled worker shortage means there are lots of opportunities in the trades for a very rewarding and challenging career.

Military, Police, and Emergency Services

There are so many benefits to joining a profession that helps people and, like many other professions, police and emergency services are facing a large number of retirements, so jobs are available. These are usually good jobs with above-average pay, stability, benefits, and opportunity for growth and transition. These are also jobs that are rarely replaceable by technology. These jobs give you the opportunity to work on a team, where you must rely on each other in ways that are intense and important. There's no way to measure the danger and the cost the risks pose to you and your family, but the rewards of being one of the important helpers in society are enormous, and there's also the status that goes with that. Training can vary from several months to several years, and often it can be done slowly, while you work or are on leave from a permanent job.

The military is also hiring. These jobs can be difficult, and the rigorous culture of discipline and order isn't for everyone. In an unstable geopolitical climate, the likelihood of being deployed to a war zone or somewhere dangerous is very real. But the sense of purpose, honor, and camaraderie is unparalleled. Members may serve in various ways depending on their country and interests. These may include the Army, Navy, Air Force, Space Force, Marine Corps, or Coast Guard, or the reserve components of these branches, including the National Guard.

There are very many support occupations in the military as well, including nurses, doctors, engineers, and lawyers. And many more civilian roles, including important tech and cybersecurity functions. The military is a big operation and there are plenty of places to move within the forces. Once you leave the forces, your experience can be very attractive to potential employers, and you'll have lots of transferable skills.

Creative Industries

Jobs in the creative industries can be very fulfilling and sometimes they pay very well. As a result, there's a lot of competition, and getting started can be especially difficult. These industries are also at particular threat from AI, with current copyright laws often failing to protect intellectual property. This was a central issue in the 2023 writers' strike. But creatives will always create, and there will be ways to make a living, but it isn't easy and probably never will be.

Andrew is a 3D modeler who is early in his career. He's a quiet guy who likes working from home, even though he knows better relationships with people will help his career. To date, it hasn't held him back, and he's been working on some very big projects, full-time with the same company for four years. This is rare since the industry usually hires on short-term contracts, often just for a particular project. When I spoke with Andrew, he had recently been laid off for the first time. He wasn't too worried since this is normal in his industry. He updated his reel with his best work and posted it on LinkedIn. He talked to the people he knows, telling them he's looking for work, since this is probably going to be how he will get his next gig. It's going to take a little longer due to delays caused by the strike, but he's ready for that. He says if it takes more than a few months, he'll take some work outside the industry, probably for a pay cut, and probably at the golf course where he used to be a greenskeeper. In the meantime, he could upskill, learn some new software, or build his management skills, but given the experience he already has, he'll find work despite how competitive the field is.

I spoke with Andrew after he'd been unemployed for three months and this time he had a different idea. He hadn't received a call for more work, so he'd done some research, talking to friends in the field and in online chat groups. He now felt that unless he was in the top 15% of his field, his job was at risk, and he wanted something more reliable. He was considering a variety of tech jobs that would offer a similar lifestyle and build on what he already knows. At the time, he was about to attend an info session for a degree in cybersecurity. He thinks he might be able to specialize in security for the visual effects industry, taking what he already knows and loves and developing new skills in a field that is growing. Before he makes any big decisions, he first needs to find out more about the jobs outlook.

Try this: *If you are drawn to the creative industries but also want stability, consider support roles such as HR, administration, technology, accounting, and legal.*

If you have always dreamed of working in fashion, film, or interior design, there's a job for you in those fields, but it might not be what you thought. You may never lead an AD100 design firm, but you could work for one. If you don't have the skills, enough talent, or an existing client base, you might start as a researcher, account manager, or administrator. This way, you learn the business, work in a world of swatches and design renderings, and use the skills you already have.

Film and other creative industries can be glamourous and profitable, but they can also be grueling and volatile. If you work in a production office in accounting or HR, you still get to be in the industry, enjoy many of the perks (like cool wrap parties), and have a stable income and regular hours.

Justin started his career in HR for an ordinary government department, but when he thought about his next job, we encouraged him to move those same skills into his dream industry. He has now built a very successful career in HR in the animation industry. He works with creatives, helping facilitate creative projects, using his people and business skills. He doesn't just do HR, he's also a project manager on shows you might have seen.

The creative industries are using AI the same as any other field. It's used for basic business processes, to speed up the creative process, and to create new things that couldn't be created before, like spectacular stunts and stellar scenescapes. Despite the magic AI can create, we still need visionaries, designers, and idea makers. Artists take new technologies and do things the rest of them could never imagine. But AI poses significant risks when it comes to protecting ideas, intellectual property, and creative content. Regardless, artists will always create — they can't stop themselves. And it's better if they can make a decent living while doing it.

Agriculture

Making a living in agriculture deserves its own book, and to be fair, there are a few. Agriculture isn't like other industries because it's fundamental to human existence; it's often done by a single family on a small scale, and it doesn't pay what it's worth. Increasingly, farmers are engaged in community-supported agriculture (CSA) where community members and restaurants sign up for weekly boxes, and they support farmers at farmers' markets.

The small-scale farmers I spoke to want a lifestyle where they can live on the land, work with plants and animals, and do something very important. To make a living, most small farmers need a spouse with an outside job, or they need a side hustle. They might also work on nearby farms, assisting with calving, shearing, machinery repair, or other specialized skills. Some work as farm consultants. Others use part of their land for a camping or special events business, or maybe a pick-your-own pumpkin or strawberry patch. On a small scale, some produce candles, soaps, skincare products, specialty food, and clothing. With a larger capital investment, some build a distillery and produce spirits, beer, or cider. Any of these things can turn into the main business with intent, skill, and some luck. It may, however, reduce food production, but everyone is entitled to make a living.

Like most everywhere else, farming is facing an aging workforce. To get started, you need land, and for most people, this means inherited land from older generations. Others work on leased land.

Climate change is going to make the industry more volatile, more difficult, and more important than ever. And as the global population continues to increase, we'll need greater output. It's likely that farmers will become more diversified in their business operations, offering more and varied products and using new technology, and sometimes old ways, to improve efficiency.

Sales

Selling products or services is still a people job, and it always will be, but this is a changing field. More customers now rely on social media and online recommendations and reviews to make their choices, so advertising and sales representatives are not as valuable, meaning there are fewer jobs there.

For real estate agents, the future is even more uncertain, because housing is more expensive than ever, meaning fewer people are buying. Nonetheless, there's still a demand for realtors in Canada and the United States. These are good jobs for people who like people, have some good analytical skills, and are willing to work weekends, pretty much every weekend, in fact. Like with any sales job, it can take some time to build a client base, but once you're established, the returns can be solid

Jobs You Maybe Didn't Think Of
• Animal care assistant
• Animal nutritionist
• Animal trainer
• Archaeologist
• Auctioneer
• Bookbinder
• Dendrochronologist
• Dog walker
• Luthier
• Park ranger
• Sommelier
• YouTuber

Like with anything else, before you make a shift to a career you maybe didn't think of, consider the jobs outlook. A difficult path doesn't mean you shouldn't do it, but it does mean you'll probably need to be good to be successful, and you'll need a good plan to get there.

Jobs Declining in Demand

There are lots of great jobs, and many fields where there are labor shortages and jobs are plentiful, but it's important to look in the right place and be aware of areas that might be more challenging. As discussed, jobs that can be replaced by AI are in the fastest decline. Think clerical and administrative roles such as recordkeepers, bank tellers, clerks, postal workers, cashiers, ticket agents, and any other date-entry related positions. Office and executive assistants are increasingly digital or offshore. A lot of loss in these areas has already happened. Social media strategists are also in decline, with AI taking over some roles and others being moved offshore. This is a bit surprising and might not be a good idea for business growth, but this is what the stats are telling us. You can often tell what's been automated or where people are still employed from the services you receive and if you can access a real person to help you when you need it.

Try this: *If you're thinking of a move to a new industry, consider its future. Is the technology landscape stable? Can you see how AI has changed it, and can you anticipate how it will change it in the next few years?*

Conclusion

There are so many jobs out there and there's one just right for you. If you're young, I encourage you to try lots of different things, and I hope you'll be working for a long time. If you're bored, frustrated, or generally unhappy in your work and thinking about a change, maybe it's time for a big change. I'm reminded of the poem by Patsy Stone, "I hate my job. I hate my job. I need the money. I hate my job. I totally hate it." If this is you, it's definitely time to consider something else.

Over and over again, I spoke with people who ended up doing work they had never thought of; it just sort of came their way, and now they wouldn't want to do anything else. One thing's for sure: a better job is more likely to come your way if you plan for it. The world is full of people who love their jobs, and you can love yours too.

Take Action

Do the following exercises and make notes in your Career Imagination Journal:

1. Ask yourself if you're in the right field. If not, use your Career Imagination and dream about something different. Dream wide and dream big.

2. Consider the future of work in your industry. Where is it headed? Do you need to do something different to keep working how you want to work?

3. If you feel your job is vulnerable to AI or automation, consider developing additional skills, like data analysis, cybersecurity or project management.

Chapter Four

THE SKILLS GAP: *Building Bridges, Filling Holes*

In all types of work, employers are reporting that they can't find enough people with the skills they need, which can be good news for someone looking to switch jobs. As long as you can commit to learning something new, there's an opportunity out there for you because you can upskill and fill that need. You can get some of these skills without formal education and even before you move jobs. The World Economic Forum reports that 94% of business leaders expect workers to build skills on the job.[vi] We also build skills in our communities, through special projects and by teaching ourselves. Regardless of where you get them, making sure you have some of these needed skills is something you can do without waiting to complete formal education or even without currently working in your field.

If you want some job security, your task is to find out where the gaps are in your industry and what you need to do to fill them. If you don't take time to upskill, you can get locked into a job or a particular way of working, making you more vulnerable to labor market changes. Even if your job is secure, jobs can get boring when you've mastered them and stop learning and feeling challenged. So, gaining new skills is always a good idea. Upskilling demonstrates a willingness to keep learning. And lifelong learning is something employers look for.

There are many ways to stand out, but one of the best ways to improve yourself (and your resume) is through building soft *and* hard skills. Soft skills that employers commonly look for are the 4Cs: *critical thinking, creative thinking, collaborating, and communicating.* Hard skills are tech skills, and in particular, a familiarity with the AI being used, or about to be used, in your industry. The ability to use and manage big data is also very much in demand. It's great if you can get these skills on the job, but you might need to take the initiative, and you might need to look outside work to develop any specialized skills. This is covered in detail in Chapter Nine.

In this chapter, we'll look at the kinds of skills employers are looking for so that you'll be more prepared and likely have more opportunities to work on your own terms, giving you the freedom to switch jobs if the one you take isn't working for you.

Try this: *Identify the common skills in demand and in short supply in your industry. Use this to help you decide what skills you should develop.*

Soft Skills

In every field, employers are looking for people with better people and thinking skills. You need to be able to do things AI can't. You can critically evaluate your own strengths and style in these areas and see what you can do to go about building your abilities. A lot of these skills are personality-driven, but there's so much you can do to develop yourself.

It's not uncommon to turn weaknesses into strengths over time. I wasn't always a good listener, and I was terrified to ask strangers questions, and now I do it for a living. It took some time, but I learned how to do these things and then to do them well.

Critical Thinking & Analytical Skills

If you're under the age of forty, you've probably heard a lot about critical thinking all the way through school. You may have these skills, but you might need to pull them out and polish them up, since complex problem-solving is increasingly important in the workforce. These are skills you need for tackling work-related challenges, including problems with people.

Our research shows that interviewers are asking new questions, and what they're looking for is evidence of creative and critical thinking. So be prepared for questions like these:

- What are you reading, and where do you get your information from?
- How do you know what you're reading is true?
- What is the last book you read?
- How did you solve a difficult problem?

Critical thinking isn't related to a particular area or discipline; it's more about how you think and how you address problem-solving. It means you can challenge assumptions, look beyond the first or most obvious answer, and get comfortable with incomplete and imperfect information. Critical thinkers puzzle through a problem and consider a variety of possible outcomes and consequences. You need to be able to examine and interpret what you find so you can make reasoned and sometimes original decisions and then be able to articulate and justify your findings in clear and understandable ways. It doesn't mean you always have to have the answer, and it certainly doesn't mean you always have to have an opinion. Developing critical thinking skills is a process, and in short, you're looking to develop your own process that will help you consider multiple perspectives and alternatives and come up with some original or not-so-obvious answers.

Try this: Develop your critical thinking skills. You can use the methods below to practice building your critical thinking skills, or you can find ways of your own.

To build critical thinking skills:

1. Question yourself and your assumptions.
   a. Become aware of how you think and how you respond.

2. Consider then reconsider your inputs.

    a. What data are you using, and where did it come from?

    b. Are there other sources?

    c. What are the alternative sources?

3. Ask questions and look for answers in new places.

    a. Reconsider how decisions are usually made where you are.

    b. Look to other disciplines and apply some of their decision-making techniques.

4. Diversify thought and collaboration.

    a. Consider alternative views and opinions.

    b. Listen carefully and actively.

    c. Reject bad ideas but assess them first.

5. Present your findings in the clearest way possible.

    a. Consider creating high-quality visuals to represent or accompany your findings.

    b. Be prepared to provide findings in short highly visual reports: one- and two-pagers.

Analytical skills are critical thinking skills that closely consider data and help you sort through facts, evidence, and information to develop sound responses. You'll make observations, collect and analyze information, and develop varied responses to inform your decisions. These skills help you generate new ideas.

Analytical skills include:

- analyzing data
- researching
- forecasting
- reporting
- interpreting
- communicating

Try this: You can practice your analytical skills by solving crosswords or other logic puzzles or participating in structured activities like debates or group problem-solving games.

Creative Thinking

Creative thinking is how we generate new, valuable, original, and innovative ideas; problem-solve; and develop solutions. It's core to problem-solving and innovation. It's not just fancy or extravagant thinking; to be effective, it requires the careful development of ideas from thought to reality.

People who are curious and open-minded, with a joy of learning and a sense of wonder, are naturally creative thinkers. They tend to be willing to live with complexity, change, and difference, as well as navigate incomplete and imperfect data. Creative thinkers still rely on existing ideas and concepts, but they use imagination, inventiveness, resourcefulness, and flexibility to develop new ideas and new knowledge. Creative thinkers are willing to experiment, take risks, test, fail, and then implement new ideas or improve on existing ideas. We all have some ability to do these things, and we build our creative muscles over time if we work at them.

Everyone has creativity; it's just expressed differently. Any mathematician knows how creative and beautiful the numbers are, even if they struggle with the words to describe that beauty. Problem-solving is a creative process, whether you're fixing a leak or filling a sales gap. You don't need to enjoy dressing up on Hallowe'en or be a wizard with Photoshop to be creative. If you've inherited a mess, you might need to be creative to clean it up.

Try this: Think of something you love doing as a creative pursuit. Notice how you use your imagination and openness to create something new. Is this something you can, should, or want to develop into a career or apply to your current career?

Michael was an events manager working on some of the biggest and most prestigious events in the world, including presidential inaugurations, political conventions, and the Olympic Games. Every event was different, with unique challenges and original personalities. He was known for integrity and honesty and was driven to complete tasks in the most direct way possible, but each one required an original response. Because Michael was also a very creative thinker, he could deliver adaptive solutions. He spent his career working in so many different cultures and environments that he never developed a formulaic response to problems. Instead, he saw a need to be nimble and adapt as required. He would say, "We must be nimble; we must endeavor to persevere." The second part being a quote from *The Outlaw Josey Wales*.

Try this: *Improve your creative thinking skills by trying something different or doing the same thing in a different way.*

Collaboration & Interpersonal Skills

For many of us, social interactions at work are our primary means of friendship, making work an important place for learning, support, and joy. Friends enhance our work lives, and learning from each other is an important way to build skills and advance in our careers.

Increasingly, employers are looking for workers who have strong interpersonal skills, exercising empathy and leadership. Work is so often done in teams, and employers and managers don't want to get involved in interpersonal conflict, but you can make sure there isn't any or resolve it neatly if there is.

Whether you like working in teams or not, treat teamwork and collaboration as a practice and address them in a methodical way. Take the time to create trust, empathy, and friendliness in your team. Perhaps the best thing to do is to *decide to like each other*, at least for as long as you're working together. When we like each other, we build trust. Sharing a meal is such a fundamental way to engage with each other in a very human and somewhat intimate way; it's one of the most human things we can do together and it's how we build relationships. These social benefits are the reasons why employers want people in the office.

Be aware of your place in the group, whether it's a formally defined team or the organization as a whole. What is your role? Is this the role you want? Can you help other people be better? If you can, it will make you better too. And work to be part of creating a positive environment. You don't have to be the most fun person at work, but you want to be part of making work productive, enjoyable, and successful. This is your role as much as anyone else's.

You can learn to see your team as a unique entity, more than the sum of its parts. What are your team's priorities? Do you want to be fast, creative, cheerful?

Try this: *Identify the qualities that are most important to your team and do your best to embody and demonstrate them but also to complement them.*

Understand not only how to manage creative friction but also how to *create* it. Encourage disagreement and explore extravagant ideas. Share some laughs along the way. Often, it is overcoming obstacles or making mistakes that leads to the most creative and beautiful solutions.

Communication

Good communication is critical in the workplace. It sets the tone and ensures everyone knows what's expected of them, which means you'll all feel more confident doing your jobs. Also, when you communicate clearly and concisely, you are more likely to be heard and to get the response you need. The rules are simple:

1. Be polite.
2. Keep it short and to the point.
3. Think about the best medium to use. Some people respond better on the phone; others prefer email. In-person conversations are invaluable for building relationships.
4. Plan your message. Then, edit your message. Ensure it is accurate and correct and has the right tone.

And always remember that the message isn't about you; it's about your audience. Consider what they already know, what they need to know, and how they might feel about your message.

Try this: Be mindful of how many emails you send. Email can be overwhelming, and people's inboxes are always full, so make sure your email is necessary (e.g., don't hit Reply All unless everyone needs to see your response.)

When you need to pass along important information that won't work in a short conversation or email, take the time to create a short summary or fact sheet, a status report, or an update, and consider a visual representation of your ideas. This is hugely valuable to your manager. It lets them know what you're doing, keeps information at the ready, shows you as professional and organized, shows you as having initiative, and aids in decision-making. Do you need to send a weekly status report?

Also have regular conversations with your boss. They need to know that you're being productive, that you're available, and that you're thinking about work. They also need to know how you feel about your job and what you want to do in the future. If you want new challenges, you're more likely to get them if you're asking for them. Maybe you'll get something like, "Let's give Amy a chance at this; she says she can do it."

Hard Skills

Employers need people with tech skills. It's a good way to distinguish yourself from other candidates when applying for a position, and it highlights your ability to learn new information and systems. Developing tech skills may help you increase your eligibility for promotion and strengthen your overall job security. Learning new tech skills also gives you a chance to demonstrate an ability to learn new information quickly and to handle complex processes. There are a lot of different ways to pick up these skills and you can start small by learning what they are.

Try this: Identify the new technology, especially AI tools, currently being used in your industry. Make a plan to improve your skills in this area, or at least to understand them better.

Tech Skills for Non-Tech Professionals

Even if you don't see yourself as a tech professional, digital tools and platforms are now woven into daily work. Emerging technologies like AI and automation are reshaping industries and understanding them can help to future-proof your career.

People in your industry are using AI. They're using it to answer questions and to create content, such as emails, reports, disciplinary actions, plans, and processes. They're using it to get organized and to solve problems. You need to be using it too, or at least to know *how* it is being used and how it can be used. Did you know you can ask AI to teach you how to use it, and that your AI will learn you, giving you better responses over time? (You might need to come to terms with how much information you want it to have about you.) It's amazing what it can do, and it's only getting better. Don't panic; the changes AI brings are not happening overnight, but they are happening now. A lot of changes have already happened because people you work with are using AI. If you're not one of those people, now is a good time to find out how to use it. AI can help you with that.

There's AI, and then there's everything else. From project management software to data analytics, knowing how to use the right technology can set you apart and may make you better at your job. For non-tech workers, there are basic skills everyone needs. You might be able to teach yourself or get the help of an online tutorial. But to build more sophisticated skills, consider taking a course.

Here is a list of skills currently in demand that could help improve your employability in the labor market or get you advanced in your current position:

- Word processing
- Emailing
- Videoconferencing
- Audio and video editing
- Data management
- Social media
- AI searches
- AI-assisted writing
- Search engines and online research
- Customer relationship management (CRM)
- Search engine optimization (SEO)
- User experience (UX) and user interface (UI)
- Analytics
- Digital marketing

Steps for improving hard skills

- Identify relevant tools: Research what digital tools are most commonly used in your field.
- Take free courses: Platforms like Coursera, edX, and LinkedIn Learning offer a range of free and paid courses in digital skills.
- Practice: Apply what you learn in real-world scenarios or side projects.
- Stay updated: Follow tech trends in your industry to keep your skills current.

Try this: Track industry trends via resources like Gartner or TechRepublic. McKinsey, Forbes, and Pew also offer up-to-date insights.

Tech Skills for Tech Professionals

If you're an experienced tech professional, you'll already have lots of competencies. Upskilling and learning new software are part of the landscape, and you're likely familiar with how to get what you need. The task then is to anticipate where the jobs are and prepare yourself to be there. You might find that you are better off developing your soft skills to complement the tech skills you're already good at.

If you're right out of school, it's harder to get a job. It's painful when you put in enormous amounts of time, effort, and money to get educated only to find that you need experience to get the job you trained for. For many tech and knowledge workers, there's a gulley between the completion of your education, and when you have enough experience for the better mid-level jobs.

You can get that experience by building your skills in one of the tech-heavy sectors, such as government, banking, education, and healthcare. After a couple or a few years, you will be better positioned to move into something that might satisfy your ambitions in a different way. Or you might have found a niche, settled in, and are happy to stay a while.

For young people, co-op positions and internships make an enormous difference, and if done right, they come with mentoring as well. Often, people need to start in basic jobs, develop their skills and demonstrate their abilities before they can move into a better job. This isn't new, but it can take longer than it used to. Getting experience managing people and developing the skills employers want is also helpful. It's worth keeping in mind that if you're twenty-five, you may well work for another forty to fifty years, so try to avoid being in a rush and build experience in a variety of areas you're interested in. It will all add up to something, and you're more likely to end up in the right place.

Ways to get experience and improve your opportunities:

- Do volunteer work
- Join clubs and other extracurricular activities
- Talk to recruiters in person or one-on-one

- Build your skills and add new skills
- Go for information interviews — people want to help other people, especially young people
- Take part-time and temporary work — while not ideal, eventually you'll land something full-time

Try this: Carefully consider if adding new or more advanced certifications and qualifications will actually add something you need and improve your career. There can be pressure to keep adding to your resume, but this can be expensive and time-consuming and may not result in a real benefit.

Conclusion

The good news is that you can learn new skills on the job, in school, at home, and in many other ways. Look around and see what skills are in demand and how you can fill that demand. Look to yourself and see what you need to better position yourself for the job you want. You can learn quickly or take your time. And you can do it while you look for new work; just make sure you put it on your resume. It helps if you've made learning new skills a habit because continuous learning is an important marker of success.

Take Action

Do the following exercises and make notes in your Career Imagination Journal:

1. Identify the skills gaps in your industry. Check online sources, check industry chat groups, and people you know. Then think about how you might address those same gaps in yourself.

2. Do a skills assessment. What skills have you gained in the last year? Which ones do you want to build next?

- You probably already have the skills that are needed in your industry, but do you have skills that set you apart?
- How skilled are you at working with people? Would a course in collaborating, management or leadership be an asset to you and your work?
- Is critical and/or creative thinking a strength for you? How do you apply it at work? Should you give those skills a workout and build some intellectual muscle?

3. Identify one skill that's in high demand in your field and that you'd like to learn or polish. Find a free online course — such as through Coursera or LinkedIn Learning — to get started.

4. Consider looking outside your current industry to places that need what you have or what you can get.

5. Consider learning a new tech skill.
   - Find out how you would develop that skill or learn that program. YouTube is often a good place to start, and Reddit is full of advice, a lot of it good, especially the career advice.

6. Consider your people and leadership skills. Would a course in collaborating, management or leadership be an asset to you and your work?

7. Is critical and/or creative thinking a strength for you? How do you apply it at work? Should you give those skills a workout and build some intellectual muscle?

Part 2

Driving Your Career

Chapter Five

CAREER IMAGINATION:

Dream It and Do It

With years of experience and from the insights I gained in researching this book, where I spoke to more than one hundred people about their careers, I discovered that people who successfully changed careers had some things in common. They all dreamed big, talked to a lot of people with good support from a few, had a (mostly) positive attitude, and didn't give up. Add it all up and this is what it looks like to succeed at work in the 2020s:

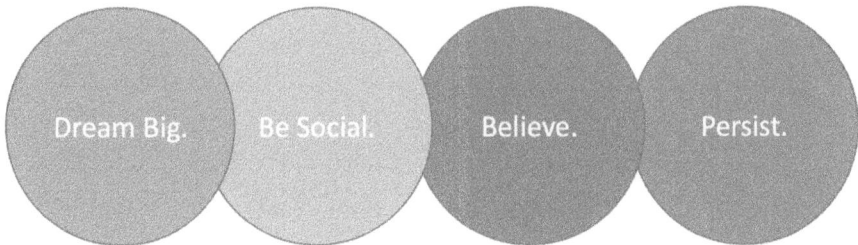

Dream Big. Be Social. Believe. Persist.

1. **Set a big goal.** And make a detailed plan to achieve it.

    If you believe and are persistent, you will get where you're going, so dream big. We call this "Career Imagination."

2. **Create a strong social network.** This will help you build skills, find work, get supported, get advanced and have more fun. Your social network can be big or small; the important thing is that it functions.

3. **Believe and be optimistic.** Believe that you can do what want to do. It doesn't have to be easy to be successful, but you need to know you can. You will adapt to change and manage risks, which will give you confidence and help you keep believing.

4. **Be persistent.** Goals can take a long time to achieve. A big part of persistence is staying focused on what you want and committing to continuous learning and skill development.

Dream It, Plan It, Do It

I draw you back to the very first question: If the sky were at its bluest, what would you be doing? The idea is that you're doing the work you feel you should be doing, the work that gives you joy and is fulfilling. Career Imagination is how you come up with what is possible for your work life, and then believe that it can be true. Think big here, because if you have a good plan and you stick with it, you're very likely to achieve your dreams, so make them what you want. And keep in mind that ordinary people enjoy wonderful careers — it happens every day.

Maybe you're an artist, and you just don't know it because both your parents are accountants. Maybe you've always had a desk job, and you've forgotten that you could be a landscaper, or you haven't yet figured out how to make a good living working in the dirt. We ask our students to think about their dreamiest job in their most admired company or organization. Usually, they don't dream big enough; they tend to stick with what they were already thinking. But sometimes, they end up with something really wonderful. My job is to help my students, and now you, achieve the wonderful by finding the job that is going to fit you best, better than the job you already have. Once you have some dreams, you can set some goals. Goals are more practical than dreams, but you need both.

Matias was studying marketing. He'd been making and selling unique T-shirts with his brother, which was a fun thing to do on the side, but he didn't see a career in it. He had thought about marketing in banking or healthcare, but he wasn't done with fashion. When pushed to dream big he made fashion retailing his goal. He made a list of the best bespoke tailors he could find and researched each one. He was ready to ask good questions and answer their questions. Then he started cold calling. On the second call he got the right person on the right day. The owner of a premium tailor and boutique in Manhattan had just decided to bring on a marketing intern that morning. They hired him on the spot, over the phone. He learned as much as he could, then took his skills and knowledge into a successful career in fashion marketing.

Dream without Borders

When you start dreaming of career possibilities, don't limit yourself to staying where you are just because you're already there. Despite how much she loved her job in higher education, Carmella knew she would have to make a change if she were to stay challenged and satisfied. She took her time, got some more education, considered her options, and waited until the right independent project came along. She left her very secure high-status job for a small startup. The work is more challenging and more satisfying, with no commute. She doesn't know if she'll end up with a pay cut or a raise. It's a risk she doesn't mind taking.

Are You Bored?

Do you drag yourself in to work and sometimes wonder what it's all for? Are you doing the same thing you've been doing for too long? Boredom can look like lethargy, agitation or irritation, and it's draining. It's a signal that you aren't doing work that you find meaningful. If you're work is no longer challenging or engaging, you might be bored and ready for a change.

J'Anna left her government leadership role because she had lost hope that the organization would grow or change; she said she knew she was "made for more than this." She looked hard, talked to a lot of people, and found a much better job in the private sector, a job that challenges and rewards her. It took close to a year of looking and thinking, and much longer if you count when she began having casual but intentional conversations with people in her field. She started with contract work and then negotiated for the right permanent position.

Whether you're looking for new work or your first job, think widely. Look around. Look at things you like and then consider the jobs associated with that thing.

Try this: Consider big changes and then scale back if a bigger change isn't really what you want or isn't possible right now. Check in with how you feel *about what you are dreaming of.*

It's important to keep in mind that many of us are likely to be working past the age of sixty-five. When you're considering a career change, take some time to consider the following:

- How far away is retirement for you?
- How much money do you need to make before you retire? (How many years of retirement do you think you need to be able to pay for?) A good financial advisor can help you with this. Your bank might provide a consultation for free.
- What are the implications for your spouse?
- How long can you keep working in the field you're currently in? Is upskilling or retraining worth the investment to get you into something you'll like better?

The answers to these questions should influence the size of the investment you're willing to make in your career in order to create the change you need. A word of caution: More than half of all people are forced to retire earlier than they planned because of health and family issues, or because they've lost their job and finding a new one can be increasingly difficult as you age.

Make Your Plan

After dreaming (which never needs to stop), the next step is to do a little research. There's usually little point in planning for a job that doesn't exist, or that is trending down and will probably not exist soon. Look into your dream job and ask the following questions:

1. Is this job available in my region? Will I need to move?
2. Do I have the skills? Or will I need to go back to school?
3. Does it come with healthcare benefits? Will it work for my family?
4. Are the jobs in this sector changing with AI, automation, or economic shifts?
5. Is there a similar or better career that is hiring and has room for growth?

It is very very frustrating to plan for a career and invest in skill development and education only to find that you have to uproot your family for the job or, worse, it doesn't exist. When considering skills, training, certifications, and education you might need for your dream job, think long-term, because this is an important investment. It might take you ten years to get everything you need, and to build enough experience, but you may then be able to spend decades doing what you love. These years are passing anyway, and you can make them really work for you.

Have you dreamed big enough?

Try this: Be aware of overeducating. Do your research. And make sure the skills you're developing are the ones a potential employer is looking for. If you take education just for the joy of it, then there are no limits. It will probably be time well spent.

After all this, take some time to reexamine your dream using this checklist:

- ☐ Does the new thing still feel like the right thing?
- ☐ Will you be willing to persevere through whatever it takes to get there?
- ☐ What would make it easier?
- ☐ Is there a similar job or career that's a better fit?
- ☐ Have you dreamed big enough?
- ☐ Would a smaller or different dream feel better?

Stay Connected

Along with your dreaming, look at how someone in that job, career, or business, or a similar one, got there. Look beyond your current life and consider what aspirational and inspirational people are doing. These might be people you know, or people you've heard of. Find out how they got where they are.

Really think about your connections, the people in your life who know you and support you. You might get some really useful advice or help from a family member or coworker who's made a change of their own.

Talk to people about your dream. And take some time to look at someone already in that job, career or business — or a similar one — and how they got there. You can also be inspired by the giants — Muhammed Ali comes first to mind, and Steve Jobs and Lady Gaga. Look especially at how they got started when they were still ordinary people. Or you can look closer to home, maybe at a parent, a boss, a colleague, or a friend.

1. How did they get where they wanted to be?
2. What education did they get?
3. What was their starter job?
4. How long did it take them to get to the next job?
5. What skills did they learn along the way?
6. When did they start their business?
7. How much money did they have to start it?

Sometimes, you can find this information in an online bio, and often, LinkedIn tells a pretty good story. But the best way, of course, is to ask them if you can. You might be surprised how much people love to talk about their work, so go ahead and ask. Most people have a mentor inside them just dying to get out. In any case, maybe you can learn something from their experience. Maybe you can model your career path on those of the people you admire.

Try this: Check in with people who know you. Ask them what they think you would be good at and genuinely consider their responses; people will often surprise you. They're likely to tell you about someone they know or something they heard about with the goal being to inspire you.

When researching for this book, I spoke with people from all walks of life. I wanted to hear how people got to their dream job, whether it was working in their hometown or on the other side of the world. Some people were working in high-status exciting places like Disney, Microsoft, the Olympics, and the White House. Even in these big places most were ordinary people, with degrees and diplomas from ordinary schools, but they dreamed big and sought out big opportunities. They tended to speak with lots of people and let their intentions be known. Some started at the bottom, the equivalent of sweeping floors, getting coffee, or parking cars. They learned about the organization and the business before moving into a career path with the growth they wanted. In chapter eight, we'll talk more about social networks, the importance of the people you work with, and how they can help you be a better worker and successfully move to a new position.

Be Flexible

Career resilience is your ability to adapt when you're challenged or when you're faced with change. It's something we all get better at with experience. Some people love change and seek it out, while others avoid it. Regardless, change brings risk, although staying where you are comes with its own risks. It's helpful to know that within a year after a career change, people generally report higher job satisfaction and better working conditions.

If being out of your comfort zone worries you, you might want to focus on strengthening your ability to meet challenges and bounce back from setbacks. Build your strengths and rely on your support network. These are the things that help us adapt.

Some people find a new career in the same field but sometimes in a different role with new or fewer responsibilities. Ben took a job in public works at the age of twenty-three, starting at the very bottom digging ditches. He's sharp and well-liked, so he moved up pretty quickly. He was still there in the same public works yard at fifty, but by then, the years were starting to feel longer. He needed a change, but he didn't want to start over with a new career. The solution for him was to switch to a different municipality. It helped that the new job had fewer people to manage, better hours, and better pay, but even without all that, he knew it was time for a change. What do they say? A change is as good as a rest.

Similarly, J'Anna started as an administrative assistant at the Olympics; it was a foot in the door at the best game in town. Her boss, Michael, believed in her and mentored her, and she rose to the challenge. She says she learned something new every day, built her skills, and learned the business of buses, cars, and egos. J'Anna served notice that she was there to play on the big field. She started to dress and act the part of a manager, which she became much sooner than expected. Eventually she was working around the globe at other exciting events.

Try this: *When people change jobs, they usually switch industries, so they rely on their existing skills and experience but in a different environment and culture. Consider a variety industries where your existing skills and experience would be useful.*

I also spoke with lots of people who had long-term, stable jobs, often working in government, education, healthcare, accounting, plumbing, and landscaping. Each one got their certification and found jobs with cultures and people they liked, where they were comfortable for a long time, without the drama (and excitement) of change.

Kevin, who worked as a biologist for nearly twenty years in the same government position, told us he stayed there because he was comfortable and could do the work he was interested in without a lot of hassle. He had a few close colleagues he worked with for years, and together they developed and delivered innovative systems for water safety. The job allowed him a lot of time left over for his family and a whole lot of hunting and fishing. But now it's time to take his pension and work independently. "I don't feel old or ready to slow down, just ready to quit where I am."

I spoke with many small business owners, some who started big and hit the ground running, and others who were more guarded, taking years to plan before making a move. Each one took risks, made mistakes, adapted, and changed to get where they are now. Jay dreamed big, using his big tech experience to start an officeless tech firm and has plans for early retirement. He felt it was a bit early in his career to go out on his own, but he left a top-flight job in Silicon Valley to do it because he also felt this was going to be the best time to get started. He'll start a family soon and life will be busier, so now was the time to take a very big risk. It helped that he was in San Francisco, which he noted "has a vibe of entrepreneurship," and external validation helped him generate the confidence and self-belief necessary to take that leap. The support of other people is such an important factor in making changes and finding success in those changes.

Other entrepreneurs I spoke to were more cautious. They dreamed for a long time, saving their money, usually paying for expenses out of pocket and eventually leaving their "day job" to pursue the independence and creativity that self-employment allows. Rena, an engineer, became an independent consultant, feeling that it was now or never to work for herself and focus on delivering excellence in the way she wanted to, without having to compromise her values. She told us, "I think there was a window of opportunity for me to focus on myself … my hands-on parenting days were behind me…. My parents were still young enough and in good health. So, I can step out from the caregiver role that has defined me since I became a mom in 2002. I prioritized family over career for many years, and it feels like I have unfinished professional aspirations." Now was the time to leave a large firm to work directly with clients.

This meant she wasn't constrained by someone else's rules, and she could do what she thought was best for the client. On her own, she is able to exceed expectations, sometimes doing things that aren't within the scope of the bid but that have value to the client.

Try this: Identify one thing that other people often say you are good at. Lean into your strengths, amplify them, and rely on them. Use your strengths to help guide both your dreaming and your planning.

Persist

Change is hard, but if you can dream it, you can achieve some version of that dream in truth. We know that some constraints can make your dreams more difficult, but you can find a version of your dream that will work for you and your family. If healthcare benefits are an issue, staying in the same industry may result in similar or even better benefits. Everyone deserves decent work, and enough of it. Your work should be satisfying, and fulfilling, and pay what you need it to. In the end, the dream needs to fit you, work within your circumstances, and play to your strengths. Dreams are not just for other people; dreams are for you. And they are more likely to come true if you have a good plan and stick to it.

The principles of looking for new work are the same whether you're looking for your first job or your fourteenth. The amount of work it will take you to get your job will depend on how much experience you already have and how big a change you are making. The amount of time it will take is anyone's guess, so be prepared to wait if necessary. This is much easier if you are looking for something new while you're still employed. I encourage you to consider big changes as an exercise and then scale back if a bigger change isn't really what you want or not possible right now.

If it's taking a while to get where you're going, find ways to keep the dream alive. A long time can feel like failure; but it's not, it's just taking time, maybe too much time, but you can keep moving in the right direction. Take a class, maybe at a local school, online, or far away. Talk to people who are encouraging and who can show you how to stay on track. Practice some of the skills you're looking to develop in your career. Look around for how you can learn more. Keep that Career Imagination fed.

Try this: Be open-minded about your abilities. Don't assume a job is out of your reach because you don't have the specific training needed for it. You can get what you need, even if it's hard to do. This is where belief in yourself is extra important.

Conclusion

Career Imagination takes some time. Spend a while — quite a while — dreaming of the impossible and rolling around in what it could look like in real life. Spend weeks, months, or even years doing this if you need to. And consider a few different ways your dream could come true. Or explore completely different, maybe even radical, ideas. If you can dream it, you can achieve some version of that dream in truth.

Over and over again, I spoke with people who dreamed, planned, shifted, and adapted. Very few were particularly lucky; most were sometimes unlucky. But all were persistent. Whatever your end goal, there are many different ways to find that job or career that is fulfilling and satisfying.

Take the time to find what feels right but know that it's okay to feel scared when you move into something new. And, finally, remember that if you have a good plan and you stick with it, you're likely to achieve your dreams.

Dreaming is something you can do while you're doing other things. For some of us, it's a wonderful pastime. You can make those dreams count and drive yourself into a new and better job. It takes most people some work to reach the place in their career they feel they should be. So many of us wander around for a long time before we get where we are really satisfied. Do your dreaming, make a plan, and then do it. Be prepared for this to take time and work, but use the pleasure of the outcome to drive you forward. Lean on friends and family; ask lots of people for advice — you don't have to follow it, but it helps to have people in your corner.

> ## Think big, because if you have a good plan, and stick with it, you're likely to achieve your dreams, so make them what you want.

Take Action

Do the following exercises and make notes in your Career Imagination Journal:

Do it today: Imagine your perfect workday. Where do you work? What do you do? Who is with you?

Do it tomorrow: Think about jobs that put you in position for the perfect workday, probably not every day, but lots of days. Write down three possible jobs and think about them over a few days. Then, decide if they are the right thing for you right now.

Do it this month: Find some examples of people doing the job you wish you had. See if you can learn something from their experience.

On reflection: Think about your dream. Is this the right dream? Do you need a bigger or smaller dream? What do you need to achieve your goal? Identify what feels right.

After all this, map out your perfect workday five years from now. What are the steps — large and small — that you will take to get where you're going?

Chapter Six

KNOW YOUR STRENGTHS:

You Need These Most of All

When planning your career, updating your resume, and talking to people, focus on your strengths — you need these most of all. This doesn't mean you shouldn't be aware of your weaknesses and address them if you can. You might get asked about them in a job interview and how you can improve them, and you'll be ready with an answer. But most people spend too much time worrying over a personality trait they're not fond of and don't have a lot of ability to change. Sometimes, what you see as a weakness is often more a matter of inexperience — and you can gain experience.

You'll know a weakness is worth trying to fix if it's tied to behavior, not personality. If it's personality, it's who you are; don't try to fix it, reframe it. "I talk too much" might be a personality trait, and, by the way, it's not a weakness. It means you're social and you like people. "I can learn to listen better" is a behavior and you can learn to do it by coming up with two or three tactics to become an active listener. Reframing the issue and building some skills can turn that thing you worry about into something you're good at or at least don't lie awake worrying about.

Try this: Identify the thing about yourself that you worry about the most. Can you reframe it? Can you fix it? If not, learn not to be so bothered by it.

What do you do when you want to be great?

Your strengths are what you need to get where you're going, so focus on what you do best.

Remember What You're Good At

Consider what you're really good at. This might be in your career, it might be cooking or being a parent or spouse. Whatever it is, you're doing it because you love it, and you love it more because you're good at it. You can ask yourself, what am I doing when I'm the best?

When answering this question, our students will say things like work really hard, continue to improve, be tenacious, and overcome obstacles. While these things are really important, and you can't be your best without them, there's something more that separates those who are excellent from everyone else. And that is to be different, and to lean into those differences.

The things that make you different are often your greatest strengths. You get noticed and maybe advanced in your career because of what sets you apart, not because you can do what everyone else can do. It's easy to hire someone who can do the basic tasks. But it's the experiences, personality traits, and peculiarities that make you special, and everyone has some unique qualities. What are yours? How do you do things differently or better?

Try this: Lean into your strengths. When you do this, you develop and demonstrate your passion, conviction, depth, and, most importantly, confidence. And even better, this is inspiring to other people. The simple answer is to do more of what you're good at.

Believe in Yourself

Once you have identified your strengths, you have to continue to *believe* them. Believing in yourself is essential, but belief needs a foundation. Own your best qualities with conviction. Find your confidence by remembering what you do well. And then practice your strengths with relish — even swagger. Ignore the qualities that give you trouble. Your belief in yourself will allow you to maintain the perseverance necessary to get where you're going. Fueling your desire for something better will keep you going.

Know that you have something to say and something to contribute. When you know this, you will deliver with conviction, enthusiasm, and knowledge. And when you do, people will listen. But in order to have something to contribute, you need to do your work. This means that you have worked towards excellence, done your research, and worked on your craft.

Believe in you. Believe. Believe. Swagger. Believe.

Josh is a one-of-a-kind fashion icon in the making. His talent alone isn't going to get him to icon status. When he gets there, it will be because of his overwhelming belief in himself, his unwavering commitment to his dream, his originality, and his swagger. His style is big, glorious, and unique. He learned fashion wasn't going to come to him; he had to go to it. He's from Calgary and bounced around all the major Canadian cities looking for somewhere with enough fashion to fit his dreams. He couldn't find work, "No fashion company in Canada would hire me or even interview me." Eventually, he said, "I just can't; Canada has no fashion scene." His swagger and his belief told him the problem wasn't him; it was the country. He had been successful with some styling at Paris Fashion Week and had been published in London; just this taste told him he needed to move. An editor in chief of an important magazine pulled him aside and told him, "Kid, you've got to move to a bigger city." He needed a place where his taste for bigger risks would lead to bigger rewards, and he just picked up and went. In only a few months, he began working steadily for Hermès, Balenciaga, and other top brands, styling at London Fashion Week, and working at a top fashion academy. He is unequivocally a success. The joy bubbles out of him, and now he says, "Give me Milan!"

Self-Doubt & Imposter Syndrome

If self-doubt is an issue for you, you're in good company; this is most of us. Imposter syndrome is a more persistent and intense version of the same thing. The research commonly says that 85% of people have some kind of self-doubt. It's hard to imagine what the other 15% have.[vii] If you're stretching yourself, dreaming big, and working to get there, then you're likely to have a few doubts. This is good; you'll be looking at risks and trying to minimize them. But if doubt is getting in your way, you should look at ways to overcome negative thinking because it could really hold you back if you don't have it under control.

Try this: Learn ways to build your confidence. You can find books and processes to help with this. Sometimes, it's a process of regular affirmations that you do yourself.

Feeling like an imposter is normal, especially when you're growing. It signals that you're stepping outside your comfort zone and challenging yourself, going somewhere new. Instead of trying to eliminate these feelings, reframe them: Self-doubt means you're learning and expanding your capabilities, not that you don't belong. You can also go back to your strengths, reexamine and then confirm them if you need to. But keep believing in yourself and hang out with people who also believe in you.

Being really good at something means you might be able to fill a gap that others can't. Our research shows that when you fill a niche, you're more employable and better able to set the terms of your employment. This takes time and awareness. Get good at the things you love, especially the things that other people aren't doing or where there's a need. What problems go unsolved? What skills are in short supply? What do you wish someone at work could do? Can you do it?

Try this: *Notice opportunities to fill a gap or add a product or service. Is this something you could specialize in?*

Liz worked for years on very large events in strategic marketing and partnerships. She worked for the Olympics, Special Olympics, U.S. Opens, Inaugurations, political conventions, and special events. It was exciting and stimulating, but insecure, with a lot of time spent unpaid between gigs. Unlike Carmella, who went back to school in her fifties, Liz took the skills she already had and created a position for herself in medical education programming, building on her previous experience. "I found a home and created a niche in that home, in an area that wasn't being paid attention to. I made that my job." She adds, "My success was in my ability to be a chameleon. I opened myself up. I didn't have any direction or mentors to guide me in doing this. I had to take chances and big risks; it doesn't always work, but this did." Liz not only has stable, well-paying work, she travels business class all over the world to the kind of exotic places where conferences are held.

Conclusion

You don't have to be the best at everything, but knowing what you do best means understanding your strengths. Usually, these are also the things we love to do most. There's little as satisfying as doing work that you do very well and love. This is often the best way to make a decent living.

When you find what you do best, you can focus on that, build on it, and learn to do it better. This is what makes you different from everyone else who does what you do. Eventually, you become an expert, and when you do, you'll have many more choices in your career. But you can also enjoy the feeling of being excellent, of knowing that you're doing something of quality. It's a good cycle that feeds on itself and makes you better.

Take Action

Do the following exercises and make notes in your Career Imagination Journal:

Do it today: Identify something you do really well. Consider how you do it and how you can do it better. You'll be considering:

- what you do best
- what you love doing the most
- what makes you different

These are your strengths. Develop, refine, and do more of these things.

Do it tomorrow: Think about when you feel energized at work. What tasks make you lose track of time? Is this what you do at work better than everyone else? Look for places that need what you do best. Consider how you can position yourself there. Do people perceive you as excellent in this way? Do you need to show them or remind them?

Do it this month: Take action. Do what you do best and apply it to your work. Then, learn to do it even better.

On reflection: Track your awesomeness. Keep a record of things you've done really well and the times you've felt accomplished, appreciated, or both. What did you do with swagger?

Chapter Seven

ACHIEVING EXCELLENCE:

Make It Beautiful

For a career to be truly fulfilling, to grow your soul, you need to be able to do it well. There's enormous satisfaction in being good at something, and generally, when you've done something well, you know it deep in your bones. Through my research, I've identified three things necessary to elevate your career and do your job well. These are the same qualities that employers look for in the hiring process and that you can highlight to set yourself apart:

- Professionalism
- Differentiation (what makes you different)
- Craft (how you do your work)

Professionalism

There are many traits that contribute to a person's professionalism, including being responsible, dependable, and respectful. Being professional can give you a sense of satisfaction and value, and it impresses others. It can be applied to anything you want to do well, especially if you're doing it with other people. Professionalism is a significant quality, and it will help you advance, giving you more opportunities. Maybe it's a different path to be successful if you're brilliant. For the rest of us, being professional, thorough, and diligent just might be enough.

Aaron is a top-tier construction framer. He often works alone because he has trouble hiring people who can keep up with him and who meet his high standards for excellence and beauty. He told us that women are taking over the trades because they're organized, reliable, careful, and they get their paperwork in. They don't crash the truck, and they show up on time. Now Aaron is the kind of guy who likes dirt bikes and beer with the boys, but he says he'd take one woman over two men any day. Maybe he exaggerates, but you get the point. Because he's as good as he is, Aaron respects the women he's worked with as professional and reliable. Regardless of who you are, our best advice is to be 10% more professional than others if you're not already.

Milton is impressive for his level of polish with a nicely pressed suit and tie, clean shoes, and his willingness to talk. When I met him, he was just about to land not one but two job offers. Yet, he was attending a job fair recruiting for people well below his skill level because he felt that it was best to make an impression in person, and he was determined to leave no stone unturned. "It's been a journey to get to this point. Patience, endurance, resiliency, and the random encouragement from a stranger [that's me!] all got me to this point." He found work in his field and is working his way to his goal. He'll need some bigger goals soon!

Steps for achieving professionalism:

1. *Show up.* And show up on time. If you aren't there, you can't get the whole story, understand the context, build the relationship, or collaborate in making the decision. In your career, be where the opportunities are, and sometimes, just be where they might be. Go to the meetings and the social events.

Show your face and let people know who you are. If you aren't in French class, you won't learn the verbs.

2. *Be timely.* Make sure you do the things you said you'd do when you said you'd do them. If people have to wait for you to complete tasks, they'll learn to do them without you. Being timely shows you care and shows respect for the people you're working with. It's also efficient.

3. *Go deep.* Be thorough, maintain high standards, and get to the heart of the matter. Do your research and fully consider the pros, cons, and risks of what you do. Then, know when to stop planning and commit to the decision. Complete the whole assignment and answer every question. If you can't be brilliant, you can certainly be diligent and thorough. This doesn't mean you have to work longer than everyone else, but it does mean you have to work thoughtfully and with care.

4. *Take advantage of what makes you unique.* Your unique qualities could be anything that sets you apart, not only from your competition, but also from the other people you're working with. What are your strengths? What can you do better than others? What do they need you to do? Be yourself, notice your strengths, and double down on them. It's your strengths that you need most of all.

5. *Be prepared.* Do your homework. Do your research, understand the context of your work, and determine what needs to be done. Have the right tools and the right skills in place. If you don't have them, you can get them.

6. *Follow through.* Do what you say you will do, do it promptly, and do it thoroughly. Don't be afraid to volunteer; don't overpromise, but do be bold. You don't have to be the leader, but don't be the one who drags everyone down.

7. *Ask for help.* We often forget to ask for help when we need it. A second opinion can be very useful in refining and confirming your good ideas, finding a better way of doing things, and saving you from costly and damaging mistakes.

8. *Give help.* You are part of a team, even if it doesn't always feel like it. What you do impacts the people around you. You have a role to play in making others stronger and when you do, you make yourself and the whole project stronger. And the people you help are likely to be there for you when you're the one needing a lift.

9. *Be respectful.* Be polite, don't let other people bother you. Be generous. Keep your cool under pressure. Be appropriate, look and behave the part, or the part you want to have.

Differentiation

What makes you different is probably what you do best. You'll get hired because you can do the job, but you're likely to get supported, promoted, or mentored because you stood out in some way. Preserve and develop your unique qualities.

What do you do best? In some ways, you are the best!

Consider who you're working with. What can you do that complements others or that others can't do? Identify problems your co-workers avoid. In what ways are you better suited for the job? What skills do you need to do it better? Being professional might be one of them. Having skills that are in demand is another, so is showing a willingness to keep learning and to get engaged without complaining.

Think creatively. If you're curious about something, you can lean into it and come to understand it in new and different ways. We hear a lot about authenticity and it's a difficult thing to define. But if you're being yourself, maybe your best self, you'll also be unique and authentic. And then you can be something that other people can't be.

Try this: What skills do you have that are hard to find? What positive feedback do you consistently receive? You can develop those qualities and do them better. This way, you can create a niche that makes you even more valuable than you already are.

Craft

Differentiation helps you stand out, but to truly excel, you need craft. When something is well crafted, all the details matter. You can see that care, thought, time, and passion went into making it beautiful. Beautiful means that your work is complete, the research is thorough, the questions are answered or at least addressed, and the end result is a thing of beauty. Something well-crafted should be as functional as it is beautiful. It will be the product of hard work, good planning, and considered execution. When you've done all this, you create an emotional impact, and every part has meaning. There's intent, purpose and thought. Be inspired by your favorite product or work of art. What did it take to make it something worth savoring? If your work is thoughtfully created, people will notice, and they'll be attracted to it.

It is in the crafting that we can go from very good to excellent. Our hearts can be seen, and we have delivered something of value, whether it be small or big. A humble wooden spoon becomes a thing of beauty when it is well crafted. It will do the same job as the one turned straight from the machine, but we feel a little different when we use it. And then maybe our soup comes out just a little better than before.

Make It Beautiful

Teresa is a world-class scientist who credits her success to the fact that she doesn't "think normally." She means that she's creative and can see things other people don't see. She adds, "I'd be better if I were more creative or challenged assumptions even more." Nonetheless, she is deeply tenacious and determined, always working to ensure her work is thoughtful and complete at the deepest level. Her former colleague, Pooneh, says, "We do weird things that other labs don't think of doing." What both these scientists are highlighting is their ability to think creatively and deliver on a unique vision. It's only beautiful once the research is sound, the questions are answered, and the work is delivered in a way that communicates. Only then is it well crafted.

Admire Your Work

Conclusion

Being professional, different from others, passionate, and careful about your work will bring you more opportunities. We're never better than when we are doing something really well. You can take pleasure in the feeling you get when your work is well crafted and when it's beautiful. And when you notice that feeling, enjoy it! You can find ways to do more of the work you love, with it becoming a hallmark of who you are when you excel.

Take Action

Do the following exercises and make notes in your Career Imagination Journal:

Do it today: List the qualities of professionalism you do best. Are there some you should work on?

Do it tomorrow: Think about how you make something beautiful. What are the extra steps you take to craft something well? Can you do this more often or do it better?

Do it this month: Begin working on one of the qualities of professionalism. Choose a measure that will tell you when you've improved in this area. (For example, *I improved my response time to messages. I put in extra effort and went to an additional event. I increased the amount of research I did to solve a problem.*)

Chapter Eight

SOCIAL NETWORKS: You Help Me and I'll Help You

Some days it's so much fun to go to work. Usually, this is because of the people we're working with or the people we're serving. Your job has enormous social value, and some of your work relationships will become friendships. It's great to work with people who support and intrigue you. These relationships can be emotionally satisfying and engaging. Yes, they'll cause you stress, but the stress is often because they matter, just like with family. For some people, their work friends are their closest friends. There's something about struggling through and solving a problem together that is binding, and the greater the intensity of the struggle, the greater the bond. For many, work friendships last for life.

Our jobs also allow us to contribute to our communities and provide us with the ability to benefit others, sometimes in lasting and meaningful ways. There's a lot of research showing that social impact has an enormous influence on job satisfaction; some research shows it's *the number one* factor in happiness on the job. Job satisfaction is partly tied to how committed we are to advancing the goals of our employer. We're far more likely to make this commitment if there's social benefit in those goals; profit-seeking alone has limited emotional appeal. Again, it's about the people. When we're helping people, it's a lot more satisfying to go to work and do it all again like we did yesterday.

The emotional and social upkeep of networks is work, and it's harder work for some than others. Thinking about your social network as part of the work process can help you be intentional and strategic about how you engage with other people. You don't have to feed your anxiety by talking to more people than you need. But do cultivate a few people in your field who can help you and who you can help in return.

Try this: To increase the social impact of your work, consider joining a workplace volunteer group or finding ways to improve processes that directly benefit clients, customers, or colleagues.

In addition to the joy good work relationships can bring to us, they are also hugely important for success in our jobs and for career development, both at our current workplace and at our next. They also mean we're more likely to get noticed, mentored, and advanced. (Look up *Social Network Theory* if you want to know more.) But you don't have to be an extrovert to have a high-functioning social network. Introverts may have a small but robust network. If you're an extrovert, you might have a large social network, and sometimes it can feel too large or it may even *be* too large. Either way, the people in your network will make work more fun and keep you company. And they will help you find jobs, help you grow, mentor you, and teach you.

Try this: Find people you can discuss your work with. You'll learn new things and build your professional social network.

Looking for Work

Your network doesn't just support you while you're at work. It's also your best resource when you're looking for new opportunities.

Scrolling job boards can be difficult and frustrating because it's too often ineffective. An estimated 70% of jobs are never posted, and as many as 80% come about through someone you know. This is why you'll hear repeatedly to get out and talk to people, let them know you're looking for work, and be specific about what you're looking for. The people you know, and the people *they* know, can help you find out which employers to seek out and which to avoid and provide you with information on rights and wage expectations. This makes building relationships and networking key to career success, but it's extra hard if you're an introvert, or new to a place and don't know anyone. Nonetheless, you need people to help you get a job and, later, to develop in that job.

Try this: *Your secondary network is almost as important as your primary network. When you're talking to someone about your work, and you need to talk to more people, ask everyone, "Who else do you think I should be talking to? Can you make an introduction for me?"*

Tim told me his network has been his most powerful career asset and that many of the opportunities that shaped his career — from consulting contracts to leadership roles — didn't come from job boards but from people who thought of him when the right moment came along. So, somehow, he needed to be present enough for them that he would come to mind when they needed someone like him. Networking isn't transactional — it's relational. It's one of the most human aspects of career building and it's hugely valuable.

Is it time to call a friend, or make a new one?

Sandy is a highly skilled computer science engineer and mathematician. He is independent to his core and despite being well educated, is mostly self-taught. Even though he generally works alone, his social network has fueled his career and expanded his skills. He has a large, closed network of similarly high-performing computer science professionals he learns from, contributes to, and socializes with. He also finds ways to communicate with the bigger world, noting that, "Having a blog has been surprisingly important. It gets me talking about things I'm doing. It helps people find me. I've got three jobs from it." So, for a self-professed tech geek, Sandy understands the importance of working with people, and he makes sure he finds them.

Try this: Talk to someone who can provide you with more information about the industry you're working in or hoping to work in.

Networking

Networking is often misunderstood as a transactional activity, handing out business cards or making small talk at events, with everyone watching the clock until they can politely leave. When it works, networking is more about building genuine relationships that can provide you with useful information, support your career growth, enrich your work experience, and create new opportunities. These are developed in many different ways and in many different places. Developing these relationships with intention and care is crucial for long-term career success. This is your network, and it doesn't have to happen at an event.

Even so, there's value in networking events, although they don't usually lead you directly to a job, so don't take your resume with you. The key lies in preparation and intent. Before attending a networking event, take a moment to be clear on why you're going. Maybe you're hoping to learn more about a specific industry. Or to meet and be inspired by professionals with a career you admire.

Try this: If you're going to an event, research attendees or speakers in advance and prepare a few specific questions that you can adapt as needed. This preparation shows your genuine interest and sets the stage for better conversations. For sure it will help you feel less awkward.

Once you're at an event, remember to prioritize listening over talking. People naturally warm to those who show genuine curiosity about their experiences, and most people love to talk about their work. You can make mental notes of interesting details and ask thoughtful follow-up questions. Try to keep the focus on the person you're talking with rather than impressing others with your achievements; it's about building a connection based on mutual interest and respect.

For some it can be easier to network online. You can do this by sending a direct message to people in your field. You'll have to do it many times and be specific in your messages. You'll be asking for information, new contacts, and coffee chats. Keep in mind that most people want to help. They need to know that you'll be grateful for their time and be amiable and willing to follow the advice they offer.

Annabelle was an immigrant, new to Canada, and a marketing specialist who gave up on online job boards after sending out hundreds of resumes. She shifted gears and started messaging people in her field on LinkedIn. Again, she messaged hundreds of people but instead of asking for a job, she was asking for a conversation, a connection. This way, she got offers for forty-eight coffee dates and went on *every* one. The result was three job offers and one successful position.

Informational interviews can be a better and easier way to build your network in a low-pressure setting. Try to keep them informal and manageable. Approach the conversation with curiosity, not as a hidden job inquiry. If the relationship develops naturally, opportunities may arise later. Your goal is to be inspired and to gain information.

Following up is where many people drop the ball. You can send a thank-you message within forty-eight hours, referencing a specific insight you appreciated. Staying in touch doesn't require constant communication. Periodic check-ins or updates, sharing an article relevant to their interests, or congratulating them on a milestone can keep the relationship going. People who have helped you love to hear when you're doing well, so send that update and thank them again. These behaviors are kind and are part of professionalism.

Networking is challenging and everyone feels a little nervous about it at times. The key is to start small and stay curious. Relationships built on trust and genuine interest will inevitably lead to opportunities you couldn't have predicted. Networking isn't about collecting contacts — it's about cultivating meaningful, mutually supportive relationships that make work more engaging and life more interesting.

Meet → Connect → Follow Up → Give → Receive → Repeat

Mentorship

A good mentor will guide, critique, and encourage you. They'll teach you, promote you, and act as a model.

Martha is an expert transportation planner for large global events. She loves a good bus, but for her, really, it's about the team. She works with very large temporary workforces, as well as highly skilled professionals. Either way, she loves leading a team and looking after her people; she's a great mentor, instilling confidence in her people and drawing out the best in them. J'Anna, again, was mentored by Martha; she told me, "So back when I was starting out (so young), Martha in my mind was this strong, intelligent woman. She led by example. She coached and mentored through her language and her actions, all while having the most fun. I feel like I am who I am because she was such an incredible female leader. She never took any garbage from anyone, and she spoke her mind."

Unsurprisingly, Martha cites good mentorship as the most important to her career development. "You need someone who believes in you, promotes you, and cares about the people who work for them." Martha and I had the same mentor, Michael, who you'll hear about at other times in this book. He was so important as a friend and mentor to so many people that he left a giant-sized, indelible mark.

As a leader, Michael was remarkable; his staff would follow him anywhere. There are many reasons why. Firstly, he was very loyal to his staff and would go to lengths to stand by them. As a result, they consistently brought him their very best work, being uniformly unwilling to disappoint him. Secondly, Michael was very gifted at seeing what people needed to do to grow, and he was willing to take the time to show them what they were missing. He did this in ways that made it easy for staff to acknowledge their weaknesses and learn new skills. Partly, he was self-deprecating and very funny, but more, he was a successful mentor by avoiding judgment. There was a sense of celebration on Michael's teams and a strong culture of respect — everyone was included. It was a point of pride that no one was left out, despite the difficult personalities that teams are often confronted with … and that Michael was particularly attracted to. This environment made collaboration with partners and other teams much easier since they, too, were drawn to that sense of joy and collaboration. Finally, there was a strong sense of trust amongst members of Michael's teams. This also translated outside the team, where others came to expect that working with Michael's team was not only fun, but that they could expect diligence and integrity.

Great mentors or sponsors don't come along every day, but you should look for them and hold on to them where you can. It's up to you to develop and maintain those relationships. Sometimes, if we stay in the game long enough, we end up helping people who mentored us. And eventually, many of us will become mentors ourselves.

Be good to your mentors and they'll be good to you.

Your Place on the Team

Collaboration is one of the top things employers want to see more of. This will never change, no matter what AI or the economy does. And being collaborative doesn't mean you aren't competitive. When you help people, they can help you. Hoarding knowledge and opportunity can get you in some very hot water with your colleagues and may ultimately hold you back. On the other hand, developing your team enhances connections and improves your own personal performance.

As good collaborators, we elevate ourselves by elevating those around us. If we make it part of our goal to lighten the burden of our colleagues, it makes everything better and easier. Part of what we're doing is being in the fight together and building trust. Over time, there's inevitably a degree of vulnerability, and when that's noticed and then protected by the people we work with, it's a powerful connector because we've been tested and shown to be trustworthy.

If this doesn't come naturally to you, ask yourself: *What do I have to offer? What is needed? How do I offer it?* If you're good at something other people aren't, this is something you have to offer. Maybe you give really good feedback. Or you keep people going when they get tired. Whatever it is that you're good at, you can share it. These things get noticed and make work more fun for everyone.

Sometimes, we work with people who are awkward; they always manage to say the wrong thing, and they never help out. These people need the rest of us; they're just not good at making that connection. It shows good leadership, as well as kindness if you can include them sometimes.

Conclusion

Working and learning are ultimately social activities. And who we work with, talk to, and enjoy lunch with matters. People are key to developing our skills and improving our knowledge and understanding of work and the world around us. And they usually make the difference when it comes to getting new jobs and advancing your career.

Take Action

Do the following exercises and make notes in your Career Imagination Journal:

Do it today:

- Consider your social network:
    - Does it work?
    - Do you need to work it better or make it bigger?
    - Do you have the people you need to help you learn and grow?

Do it tomorrow:

- Identify someone you'd like to talk to about your work. Make a plan to talk to one or two people.

- If you don't know the person you want to talk to, see if you can get a friendly introduction to them from someone you do know.

- Reach out to a previous mentor or colleague and let them know what you're doing these days. Staying in touch keeps you top of mind and builds your network.

- Consider the most important people in your professional network. How can you support one of them this week?

Do it this month:

- If your social network needs some work, join a club or take an interactive class. It can be in anything, and it helps a ton if you're interested in what happens there.

Chapter Nine

UPSKILLING: Learning More, Working More

If you're one of those people inclined to ongoing learning, you're likely to have better success in your career. With learning, you can distinguish yourself from others and become a more desirable candidate. You might not use your new skills right away, but if you have them in your pocket, you'll pull them out eventually.

New skills give you more options and you're likely to advance more quickly at work. I saw this repeatedly with the people I interviewed. When they developed their skills and got more education, they were more likely to be able to develop their career in the direction they wanted. Ongoing learning gives you confidence and builds your belief in yourself because you're regularly achieving something and noticing growth in yourself. When you're learning, you're accumulating knowledge and abilities, which builds noticeable progress and gives you the tools to contribute more. With new skills, you will probably enjoy your work more and feel that your efforts are recognized and your time is well spent.

Try this: Consider if you have started to stagnate at work. When you stop learning, it might be a sign that you've outgrown the job and it's time to move on to something more challenging. Some people put this energy into a hobby or in their community, but eventually your disinterest will probably take its toll at work.

When you're progressing and learning, you don't get locked into particular ways of working that can limit you in the job market. If your job is challenging, you'll learn and upskill on the job. But you can learn and upskill at home and in your community as well.

There are a lot of different ways to improve your knowledge and skills. Volunteering is great for this and is an excellent way to develop skills. A friend or mentor might be able to share enough to get you started and point you in the right direction. If you're a self-learner, you've probably already picked up a lot, maybe with help from YouTube or through reading, doing, and figuring out. Online videos are a good way to learn new software, for instance, and are usually provided by the software developer for free. Podcasts can help you think about soft skills like leadership and communication that employers are finding in short supply.

Try this: Before you commit serious time to learning something, research how the discipline has changed with the advancement of AI and other technologies. You may need different tools now. This is true in bookkeeping, for instance.

Transferable Skills

When you're looking to make a work-related change and you need to get something going, in addition to talking to people, take a look at your skills. You likely have some more skills to add to your resume. The big tasks you can do are probably already on it, maybe "skilled negotiator" or "proficient in Adobe Creative." But there are a lot of other things you can do that you probably haven't identified.

Try this: When showing off your skills on a resume, use words like "manage," "collect," "communicate," and "develop." If that conference couldn't have happened without your participation, or that account got brought in with your help, use words like "contributed to," "collaborated with," and "key participant of."

Don't discount things you've learned at home and in your community, often informally or on your own. You might be conversational in Spanish, a bitcoin trader, or able to cook *and* serve a five-course meal without breaking anything. Include these things on your resume, as they show a willingness to learn, persistence, and skills mastery, and perhaps also a commitment to excellence in a particular area. They also show a well-rounded character. Use words like "mastered," "specialized in," "skilled in," and "sophisticated understanding of."

Jerome had a successful stained-glass business which was partly a skilled trade and partly art. It was satisfying work, and he had lots of customers, but eventually, the market was flooded by a big-box retailer, and he needed to adapt. Without a plan, he wasn't able to take the best of what he loved about making stained glass and turn those skills into something that was in demand. In Jerome's case, these were an artistic eye, fine detail work, welding, and business acumen.

With a little bit of guidance and some good planning, you can identify your transferable skills and apply them where they can earn you a decent living. With some good marketing and a little upskilling, Jerome might have been able to move to the higher end of the market, somewhere a large retailer can't satisfy, or into metalworking, perhaps, something requiring fine detailing. Jerome switched careers altogether, and while it worked out fine for him, he might have been able to keep building on his passion and getting paid to do it.

Clifford has a master's in human resources management and loads of hotel experience, so it seemed a natural fit to look for work in HR within the hotel industry. He learned that hotel chains centralize their HR at head office, not spread out across the country. Unless he wanted to relocate, and move his family, he would have to look for work in another industry. He decided not to move, which turned out fine, because most employers valued his education in HR. His hotel experience wasn't wasted either, because a lot of it is relevant to other large employers in the service sector, retail, or passenger transport, for instance.

Filling the Skills Gap

Everyone has things they can learn that will either make them better at the job they have or allow them to move into a new one. Maybe you're trying to work around your skill gap or hiding the hole. But what would it take to fill it?

Also, consider the skills that employers are having trouble finding in their employees. Employers have said over and over again that they need more people with the 4Cs: critical thinking, creative thinking, collaborating, and communicating. They also state a need for more technical skills — in particular, an ability to use AI. Do you have these skills? How much effort would be required for you to learn these new things?

Try this: *Do a skills assessment that considers the skills you have and the skills that are in demand. Can you bridge that gap?*

Formal Education

Sometimes you'll require formal education to make your biggest dreams come true. There's as much to be gained in the process of thinking, researching, practicing, and problem-solving as there is in the content learned. You also develop persistence and commitment, and it should prepare you for complex tasks at work. Some fields, such as healthcare, engineering, and accounting may require you to stay up to date through certified coursework.

On the downside, formal education is expensive. Beyond tuition, it costs you time and lost wages, so think hard before you commit to it. And sometimes its value is overinflated. As a whole, the North American workforce is overeducated with as many as 90% of people saying that they have more education than they need to do their jobs, so proceed with caution. If cost is an issue, and for most it is, consider part-time schooling. Perhaps work full- or part-time in a relevant field so that when you graduate, you have some experience and connections, as well as your credential. See if your employer is willing to help you with some or all of the cost of your tuition. Often, it's worth it to them to keep you and to help you into a more significant role with them, especially if they recognize a skills mismatch. They will understand the risk to them that you might leave when you graduate and might require you to make a longer-term commitment to them.

Also carefully consider the cost of the school you wish to attend. A mid-ranked school with a good reputation is likely to provide you with an excellent education, especially at the undergraduate level. If you can get in to an elite school, is it worth it? If you and your family can afford it, or you qualify for student aid and scholarships, it can provide you with excellent opportunities, including a network of peers that could enhance your career in many ways. If you factor in the cost of student loans, elite schools are very often not worth the cost. If you invest the money you save by going to a less expensive school, you're likely to come out far ahead in both the short and the long term by going to the good school rather than the great one.

Do you need an advanced degree?

Before committing to an advanced degree, consider the pros and cons with respect to a number of factors including cost, networking potential, and skills and knowledge to be gained. We frequently see people jump from an undergraduate program straight into a master's, but it's often best to gain some experience first. This way you make a more informed choice of which program to take and you have some knowledge that will help you complete the program better.

Getting a master's degree can be a powerful way to enhance your knowledge and expertise. It's also a credential required for advancement in many professional jobs. People often start with a Master of Business Administration (MBA), which is a generalist degree and does not always have the same value as something that is more specialized. Options range from a "quickie" master's degree from an online school to one at an elite school. You can choose to complete a general degree or a highly skills-based degree like urban planning, public administration, data analytics, or automation, at any school.

When I took my MBA, I had no idea what I wanted it for other than to round out the soft skills I had learned as a high school teacher.

An MBA is very general, and for years, I wished I'd gotten a master's in something specific that would have given me a particular skill set. The MBA allowed me to get a number of very good jobs I wouldn't have gotten otherwise; it removed a ceiling if nothing else, but in time I needed more specific skills to be able to do the work I wanted to do. Then, one day, I did what I had long wanted and got a second master's in social science research. I thought and planned and replanned every day for two years before I could see where I should go. Knowing that life can get in the way and the current window of opportunity might close if I waited too long, I took a leave from work and got on with it. I chose an elite school in London, England, partly for the depth of learning, and partly for the adventure of living in a great and global city. And here we are, this book is in part born out of the work I did in London. I didn't do it to make more money — I probably won't — but I'll likely stay in the workforce longer and more happily, so in that way it was a good financial decision.

A PhD is an enormously challenging endeavor and likely provides you with an impressive body of knowledge and certainly an impressive credential. It's an awesome achievement. But is it worth it? If happiness is a factor, it might not be. If salary is a factor, it might not be. You might even find that you're often considered overqualified for a job. Too often people pursue a PhD because they're comfortable in academia and lack experience in the non-academic workforce. If you're hoping for a job in academia, you should first consider the prospects in your field. As with any job, look for postings and find out how hiring is done. Tenure track jobs have always been difficult to secure, but with cuts to higher education and ever more people with PhDs, they're more difficult than ever, especially if you haven't graduated from an elite school.

Try this: Consider that a PhD will cost you a lot in time, money, and lost wages, so before you start one, be sure it's what you really want to do. If you pursue an advanced degree for the love of knowledge, completing a PhD is worthwhile, but be aware of the limitations when applying it in the workforce.

Informal Learning

Regardless of our age or stage of career, the vast majority of learning we do is informal. Almost everyone is regularly involved in some form of informal learning, making it an iceberg of untapped and unacknowledged skills. We learn while we're working at home, through volunteer work, and other unpaid work, as well as when we're doing hobbies. Then we take these skills to work. On the job, the majority of adults under twenty-four gain their most important workplace knowledge from older co-workers, while the majority of those over forty-five draw on their own experience and independent learning used at work but not necessarily *learned* at work.

The more formal among us refer to teaching oneself as auto-didacticism. Whatever you call it, it's valuable, and most of us are doing it all the time. Did *you* work your way through Julia Child's *Mastering the Art of French Cooking*? If you did, you learned a lot of valuable skills you will use at work, even if your work has nothing at all to do with cooking. Think of the math you used. And the organizational skills you developed. Did *you* teach yourself to fix the lawn mower?

Volunteering is a wonderful way to pick up new skills and meet lots of people, some of whom may have valuable knowledge that might help you in your career. You'll learn some things, and maybe you'll even become an expert in some things. You'll make new friends and maybe open a few doors. And you'll likely feel good about helping out in your community. If you have time, think about where you could volunteer, make some new friends, and learn or further develop your skills.

Try this: Look for a volunteer opportunity where you can build new skills and/or develop the skills you already have. The skills you'll learn might not be immediately obvious, and you don't have to apply them to work right away. It all adds up to something.

In addition to offering formal credentials, most universities, colleges, and school boards offer short courses and micro-credentials in a variety of areas. These can take just a few hours or a few weeks and may offer badges to validate that you acquired a specific skill. They also show that you have an interest, commitment, and willingness to learn more. Through them, you might be able to save the cost, time, and trouble of a more formal education. Micro-credentials are good for skills like marketing, communications, software, leadership, and human resources. Good places to get them are:

a. School boards
b. Community colleges
c. Universities
d. LinkedIn Learning
e. Other online schools

Remember Vaneese, who has a plan to sell perfume under her own name but needs to learn more about the perfume market so she can successfully sell and distribute her product? She has some good options for learning how to do this. She can take courses at little to no cost at her local school board, community college, or career center. She can take an online course through LinkedIn Learning or somewhere else, but wherever she looks for this advice, it should be somewhere with a known reputation that doesn't charge much money.

Basic business skills are well known to many; lots of people can teach them, so learning them shouldn't cost you a lot. You don't need to pay a consultant to teach you; that consultant is probably also teaching at the college, and you can get the same information much cheaper, even if you have to take the bus to get there.

If you're starting a business and you're new to it, you *must* take some basic business courses before launching your own company; there's so much to take in. You need to learn some marketing, bookkeeping, taxes, and regulation, or you're at risk of unnecessary mistakes. You're going to make mistakes, but you can limit them by educating yourself. Now is as good a time as any to get started. Look around for options. Public institutions are usually better than private ones. For one thing, they often pay their instructors better and charge less. If you're lucky, you can find a mentor who is willing to teach or support you.

Are You Ready to Upskill?

For some people, it can take some planning and some getting ready before they can begin upskilling. Here's a quiz to see if you're there yet or you need to do a little more sorting out first. For each question below, answer high, medium, or low. If you answer medium or high for most questions, you're probably ready.

If you answer low for a number of questions, you might need to make some room in your life for upskilling. This could mean making some changes, or it might just take some time to get a few things sorted out.

Take this quiz to see if you're ready for upskilling.

	Answer high (H), medium (M), or low (L).	H	M	L
1	How excited are you when you think about the new thing you want to do?			
2	How much time do you spend thinking about doing the new thing you want to do?			
3	Are you able to make some time to upskill?			
4	Do you have some money to pay for tuition or course fees?			
5	Are you willing to take the time to continue to develop your skills *after* some training, education, or upskilling?			
6	Are you optimistic about your ability to make something new work? (We call this achievement motivation.)			
7	In general, what is your tolerance for risk?			
8	In the last ten years, have you continued to learn new things?			
9	How much would the new thing improve your life?			

In an act of courage and optimism, at age sixty-eight, Michael moved across the country to get an MBA. He knew he had some things left to learn and he wasn't done working yet — that was the plan, anyway. Sadly, he passed away just as he was starting it. It seems pretty likely that Michael was the oldest among his fellow students, but still, an advanced degree was a pursuit worthy of his time, despite his long and storied career to date. In particular, Michael needed to "manage up" better. The people Michael reported to were often intimidated by him since his experience and confidence were so often greater than their own. Michael would also have benefited from better marketing and communication skills so that he could advise his superiors and their peers in a way that was as deft as he advised his own employees. Despite his age, these new skills could have helped him end his career in an even stronger position.

Conclusion

If you keep learning, in ten years, you'll be an expert. Or is it 10,000 hours? You get the point. We're learning all the time and gaining new competencies. Acknowledge these, know you've got them, and put them on your resume. Identify what skills will help your career and figure out how to get them. Be careful of too much formal education. In any case, your desire to keep learning is going to help you at work and in your career. But it's also going to keep you engaged in the world and increase your satisfaction with whatever you're doing.

Take Action

Do the following exercises and make notes in your Career Imagination Journal:

Do it today: Take the upskilling quiz to see if you're ready to get started.

Do it tomorrow:
- Think about what skills you're missing and what skills your target employer is looking for.
- Identify three skills that would help you land a better job.

- Then, think about what it would take to develop those skills and explore upskilling options. Take some time to consider how big a commitment you need and are willing to make. Is a degree in your future or will YouTube get you what you need?
- Learn one new thing related to your work today. Or one new thing that has nothing to do with your work that you enjoy.

Do it this month: List all the ways, big and small, that you can learn the skills you need. Talk to two or three people who have the skills you want. How did they get them? Do they advise a different path?

Chapter Ten

OVERCOMING OBSTACLES:

Keep Your Chin Up

Looking for work can take a really long time. The U.S. Bureau of Labor Statistics says that, on average, it takes about five months to find a new job. You might be ready for that, but if it takes longer, it can be painful and demotivating. If you're out of work, you have no choice except to keep going. You might take a break, and you might settle in the short term for something other than what you want. If you do this, you can still stick to your long-term plan and shift to the right thing when it comes along.

It's easier to find a new job if you already have one. Being proactive and anticipating a job shift makes sense if you see you're in a volatile environment. If you think a layoff could happen, or you've reached a plateau and need to make a change, you can start to prepare in advance, giving yourself a considerable advantage.

Try this: *If you think a job change is coming your way, start engaging your social network and consider upskilling. Stretch your Career Imagination and do some research about who is hiring.*

It's important to leave your old job the right way. Give lots of notice (at least a month if you can) and leave on friendly terms. You may need or want to come back. This is especially true if you're working with a mentor or colleagues you'd like to keep connected to after you leave. Jay gave two months' notice when he left LinkedIn after seven years (his first seven years in the workforce). The CEO sent him a personal note when he did, saying he'd be welcome back anytime. *Nice!* Obviously, Jay was very, very good, and obviously, he left in a good way.

Statistically speaking, your next job is probably going to come through someone you know. As discussed in earlier chapters, talk to people who do what you do, or what you want to do. You don't need to outright ask someone for a job; that can be hard and not always effective. But when you talk to someone, you can learn from their story, and you might ask them where they think the jobs are and who else you could talk to.

Try this: Ask each person you talk to for at least one person they could connect you with and one place they think might be hiring. Not everyone will have an answer, but some will be able to help you. Others might come back to you later when they think of something helpful.

Do What You Want to Be Doing

When you're looking for work, it matters to keep doing what you're good at. This behavior is really underrated. Remind yourself what you're good at, and keep at it, in your homelife and at work. You'll get even better, and you'll probably meet people doing what you do when you're excellent. And those are connections that could lead to a new job.

Try this: Remind yourself what you're good at. Focus on it and do it, paid or unpaid.

It's so satisfying to do what you want to be doing, even if you aren't being paid for it. Remember, volunteering is an excellent way to hone your skills and to meet people — and maybe someone will see what you can do and think, "I might have a job for this person." We're not advocating giving your labor away for free on a large scale, like in an unpaid internship, but contributing to your community has multiple benefits, and some of those benefits are directly for you and your job search. If you keep using the skills you've developed, keep them sharp, develop new ones, and build your body of knowledge, you'll be in the right place. If you're excited by it, you'll talk about it and be around other people who are doing the same thing you love. Eventually, you'll be in the right place at the right time. This could lead to good things for you. And it will help with your mood, which will help with your search.

Try this: *Practice doing what you trained to do. Identify how you can do this on your own.*

Believe some more.

If you love programming, then write code. Write code that you love and is experimental. Be prepared for it to fail. Figure out how to fix it. If you like research, then research something that gets you fired up. Use your training, do it thoroughly, and keep going. Eventually, you'll build a bigger body of work and can identify yourself as having expertise in an area that before was just an interest. If you like marketing, study innovative campaigns, or create a mock campaign of your own. If movement is your thing, focus on a part of the body or the machine and learn it better. Learn it deep into the tissue. Deep-focused learning is energizing. It helps you become an expert and can give you a new perspective on what you already know.

Try this: *Add what you're working on to your resume. Use terms like "currently learning" or "recently created." A recruiter or potential employer might ask you about it, and you can speak to it with confidence and enthusiasm or maybe a whole lot of curiosity. Curiosity is very attractive to employers; it shows you like to learn.*

Obstacles: Health, Family, and Other Immovable Objects

Sometimes we get stuck. We know what we should be doing and what we want to be doing, but we just don't do it. There are lots of reasons why people procrastinate, but the best advice we ever got on procrastination was to pick one thing, even if it takes one minute, and do it. Just get started on something. On any part of the task, maybe the easiest part, just start. You can take a break after five minutes. Maybe begin with something small and something you like to do. You might just need a push to get over the hump. Maybe meet someone for a chat. The right words can be very motivating.

If something bigger is going on, you might need to change your mindset. Try dreaming, but be specific about it. Consider moving cities or industries, for instance. Get your Career Imagination working. You can also talk to a professional about patterns that are getting in your way.

It's helpful to break your job search into tasks. Don't set out to find a job in a day. And don't try to meet new people all day or even every day; you'll be exhausted by lunchtime. Try to meet one or two new people in your field at a time. You don't have to engage for a long time, maybe half an hour at a time. Keeping it manageable will keep you going.

Try this: *Write down one thing you want to accomplish today, even if it takes you only five minutes to complete. Maybe it's completing a skills assessment, making a list of the skills you want to develop, or researching the industries that are hiring. Getting something done, even something small, can give you a sense of accomplishment and motivate you to keep going and do something bigger.*

Often our roadblocks are things we can't move — very real constraints like health issues or family situations — that make job hunting and working challenging. They come to most of us at some point like they did for me, raising kids on my own. Sometimes, there's no choice at all. If you have health issues or a disability, you might feel limited or stuck in your current job or need adaptations you don't currently have.

One of the best things you can do is be candid with your employer about your constraints. First be clear about what you need and then try to be collaborative rather than demanding in finding a solution. If you can't get what you need in partnership with your employer, then be more assertive. Look for adaptive solutions. This might mean working from home more often, taking short breaks more often, or using technology to support you. You can do some research to see how other people are working within similar constraints. An online chat group might be a place to start. If you need to, look for a better employer. It might not be easy to find the right fit, but when you do, they should be happy to have you. Employers who accommodate their workers often find they are rewarded with great loyalty and added effort.

Try this: *Sometimes, when we're first looking for new work, we stop and wait for a response from someone, but you can lose some valuable time doing this. It's okay if you have to choose between two things or if you say yes to something and then something better comes along. You can figure that out if it happens. There are worse problems.*

Career Building for Immigrants

If you're an immigrant whose credentials and experience aren't recognized in your new country, your dreams are more complicated. It's a painful and unfortunate position and there's no easy outcome. The North American labor market relies on foreign-born and educated professionals to fill employment gaps. Nonetheless, in 2022, more than two million highly skilled immigrants in the United States were either unemployed or underemployed. In Canada, this rate is decreasing, partly due to more rigorous screening before immigration and partly due to efforts to increase approvals of foreign credentials, but it's still a lot of people.

There are a number of reasons immigrants have trouble securing work equal to their education and experience, including not having their foreign education and credentials recognized, not knowing where and how to look and sometimes lacking cultural literacy and or language skills. And let's be honest, unconscious bias or outright discrimination may play a role as well. People like to hire people like themselves. If you're a hiring manager, check yourself — you could be missing top candidates because they aren't what you expected or who you normally hire.

As an immigrant, you have some limited options. The hardest thing is getting your credentials recognized if you can, and this will depend in part on how similar the education systems are in the two countries. While legislation is progressing so that foreign credentials are more easily recognized, waiting for your new country to do this isn't usually feasible; it can take a long time and there are no guarantees. And if they aren't recognized, you must redo your credentials to work again in the same position, which might mean redoing some or all of your education. Alternatively, you can choose a new profession. This is the difficult truth.

Build Your New Social Network

When you left home, you also left your social network and now you are tasked with rebuilding it. Just like with anyone building their social network, you can start with one person at a time. You can ask where to look for jobs, but you can also ask *how* to look for jobs. Ask about how people get hired, what an interview here is like, what hiring managers are like, and about anything you should look out for or avoid. Give people a chance to think about their response since this isn't something they think about every day, but they may well have useful insight for you. Also, ask little questions like how late do people work, how do they communicate, how do meetings work? Ask people within your community but also outside it. What they tell you might not immediately resonate, but give it some thought so you can piece together what they've told you into a picture you can see. Then, ask someone else. It will take a few people to get a clear picture.

Each time you speak with someone, be honest about what you're looking for and listen honestly to their response. This will also help you ensure you're using the right terms and can help you build your cultural literacy. The people you talk to will probably also be interested in where you're from and what jobs are like there, so share your story as well. The people you talk to might know someone else who could be helpful, so you can ask for introductions too. This is how we build a social network, one person and one question at a time.

Language & Cultural Literacy

The factors that are most within your control are your language and social skills. You can take language courses and mix with more people in the country you've immigrated to, especially those outside your immediate community, so that you can build the communications and cultural literacy skills that make employers comfortable. This means understanding the values and customs of the average local and being able to reflect those to a potential employer. If you do this in a variety of environments, you build some range to your experiences and can become familiar with cultural touchpoints. The more familiar you are with the culture you're trying to find work in, the more relaxed and confident you will be. And confidence is a crucial quality for anyone looking for work. You can take a course in cultural literacy as well, but you'll want to take it from a reputable organization; it shouldn't cost much, but if it does, it might not be the right thing. Be wary of promises that seem too big to be true.

Ways to improve your cultural literacy:

- Read the local news. Try to identify values inherent in the issues.
- Go to museums, concerts, and other cultural events.
- Learn about medical and scientific practices and beliefs.
- Take a workshop.
- Take a cooking class.
- Spend time at parks, restaurants, and other places locals go.
- Talk to local people, especially those who've lived all or most of their lives where you're now living.
- Volunteer with an organization serving a local crowd.
- Travel around the local area.

Building language and cultural language skills can take a long time, but you can occasionally take a look back and see how far you've come. Did you know *that* six months ago?

Reflection — A Necessary Step

From time to time in your process, check yourself. Ask yourself if you're doing the things you know you should be doing. Consider:

- Am I *exercising my skills,* doing the things I love the most and I do the best?
- Am I *volunteering* or in other ways using my skills and being with people?
- Am I *improving my skills* or adding new ones? How far have I come?
- Am I *talking to people* and being open with them about what I'm looking for?
- Am I *listening to what they say* and taking action on their suggestions?

When you get tired, you'll need to take a break, but then you'll get up and keep going — you always do.

If you're genuinely doing the right things to find the right work, keep doing them and, on occasion, ask yourself:

- Am I looking in the right place? Is this industry hiring right now?
- Have I spoken to the right people?
- How's my attitude?
- Do I need more education or more skills to get where I'm going?

In your search, identify what motivates you. What gets you energized and *determined*? Use that.

Try this: *Polish your Career Imagination. Consider rethinking where you're looking or what you're looking for. You might decide you're going to stay the course, or you might make a shift.*

If you're frustrated and angry and you can't shake it, then see if you can use those feelings to drive yourself forward. If not, it might be time you settled for something less than what you want while you keep looking. Being angry is going to keep you in a bad loop and other people will feel it. You need to do whatever you can to break that loop. It might mean polishing your Career Imagination and thinking about things in a different way. It might mean looking in a different geographic region or at a different industry. At this point, you probably need to change your process or change your parameters. Maybe things aren't moving for you because it's not really where you want to be. Are you looking in those places because you think you *should*? Or because that's really what you want to be doing?

Repetition in your process can be frustrating, but it's necessary. You may need to go back and talk to the same people again. This time, you can ask new questions. Keep busy, practicing what you love. Take some breaks and do things that make you happy. Hobbies are good for this.

When you've been job hunting for a while, it's hard but essential to keep your mood up. This is why doing what you want to be doing, even if you're not getting paid for it, is so important. You'll feel strong with a sense of satisfaction, and you're going to need that. It will put you in the way of the right people, and they'll see you doing what you're good at.

Try this: *Find the people you need. It's helpful to spend time with people who make you feel good about yourself and what you can do. Do what it takes to maintain persistence and stay confident.*

Conclusion

Looking for work is hard. Whether you already have work or if you're out of work, it helps to keep your skills sharp and improve them or get new ones. It helps if you're using the skills you trained for, doing what you love to do and what you do well. This will keep you in a better frame of mind *and* help you continue to build your skills. And finally, this again: Your social network is likely to be the most help of all to you. You can let people help you, and you can let people encourage you, or even comfort you. One day, you can help them.

Take Action

Do the following exercises and make notes in your Career Imagination Journal:

Do it today: Identify what you really want to be doing. Can you find a way to do it even if it's not paid work?

Do it tomorrow: Find some ways to keep doing what you're good at and what you love. You might volunteer, you might teach, you might do it at home.

Do it this month: Polish up your Career Imagination, reflect and think about alternatives. Are you looking for the right thing in the right place? If not, is this an opportunity to change some things and achieve a dream?

Chapter Eleven

THE PLAN: *Come in with a Problem, Leave with a Plan*

A plan is a series of steps laid out in order so that they can be followed to a successful conclusion, leading you to just where you want to be. It's a map that leads to something, hopefully something valuable. It's pretty daunting to set a goal (I want *that* job) without breaking down the path to getting there into manageable chunks. Ideally, your plan is tailored to you, your dreams, your values, and your family. It begins wherever you are today so you can get where you want to be tomorrow. (Note: there is much more detail on developing a plan in the accompanying workbook.)

Your plan needs to consider a few important things:

- where employers are hiring
- what skills they're looking for
- what skills you need to gain or polish

If you're headed in a direction that is different from what the market is asking for, you'll have some additional steps to create, or at least demonstrate, the demand for what you have to offer. Either way, you can drive your career in the direction you want. Then you'll arrive in the right place with the right expectations and the confidence you need. Here's how you can do it:

1. Observe Your Context

- Do a survey of who in your field is hiring and where they are.

- Consider alternative industries. For example, if you've been working in government, you might switch to healthcare, parks, or transportation. If you've been working in big tech, you might switch to education. A new industry might even give you renewed energy and a new scope for creativity. If you feel that your field might be vulnerable to technological, global, or economic changes, then look ahead and see if you need to make a shift.

2. Exercise Your Career Imagination

- Do your dreaming, exercise your Career Imagination to dream boldly and creatively to consider your options. If the sky were at its bluest, what would you be doing? What would make you feel like you were doing the work you should be doing?

  a. Consider how you like to work. At home? For yourself? In a team?

  b. Talk to people who are doing things you admire. Ask them and others what they think you should be doing. Ask them for their thoughts on what it would take to get there. People love to talk about their work, and more people love to help someone who is genuinely interested.

   c. Consider the skills, training, certifications, and education you might need to do the dream job.

   d. Consider what you do best and focus on your strengths; you need these most of all.

3. Assess Your Skills

- Identify the skills you have, the ones you've learned at work, as well as the skills you've learned at home and in the community. Skills picked up informally get used at work every day.
- Identify the skills you need. Are your current skills the ones employers are looking for? Do you need to upskill? Is what you can do reflected in your resume?

4. Write Your Plan

- Clarify your goals. Identify where you ultimately want to end up. You can set some short-term goals that will lead you there if you're not likely to get there all in one step.
- Draw up a step-by-step outline of the skills, people, and experience you need to get where you're going. Include self-reflection, measurement, and continuous improvement. Be realistic about how much time it will take to get the job you really want. You don't want to get demotivated by unrealistic expectations, but be sure not to make them *too* realistic; that can also be demotivating.
- Consider the following:

   a. Do you need to take other work while you look for the right thing?

   b. Do you need to upskill?

   c. How long will it take to achieve your dream?

- Build addressing challenges and obstacles into your plan. What will you do if it takes longer than expected to get where you're going? What will you do if you start to feel frustrated or even hopeless? Work on your resilience and adapt as necessary. Keep the dream alive. Consider taking or teaching a class. Use the skills you want to be using in your work.

5. Talk to People

- Work your social network and build this into your plan. While you're looking for work, you could set a goal of talking to someone new once a week. You can also go back again to the people who are supportive and encouraging. Everyone knows what it's like to be looking for work. And most people want to see you succeed and are willing to be supportive along the way. When you take a new job, don't forget to thank and update the people who helped you.

6. Believe in Yourself

- Belief and confidence are going to get you through this journey. Tap into your confidence by noticing what you're good at and then doing just that. Then, practice those things with relish and swagger. Keep doing it. Mastery takes repetition.

- When believing gets hard and the process is taking too long, find ways to keep the dream alive by doing things you're good at and talking to people who are motivating. Take a break if you need to.

7. Measure Your Progress

- How will you know if you're on track, moving in the right direction, or when you've got where you're going? Set milestones and check them against your goal so you can see if you need to shift, adapt, or make a new plan.

- You'll learn when to be realistic and when to keep the big dream alive. Sometimes it takes longer than you want, but I encourage you to always keep the big dream alive until you achieve it or you get a new big dream.

8. Continue to Improve

- Looking for new work is difficult, especially if you're not currently in a job. Build in a process of self-reflection. Periodically take a step back to see if you are where you think you should be. Reconsider your process and adapt if you need to; stay the course if you don't.

Believe in you. Believe.
Believe. Swagger. Believe.

I met Ryan when he was working as a server at a large and very popular brewhouse. Like most servers, he saw this job as a holding place to pay the bills. He had a dream to be a pilot and started school for it, but the dream was disrupted. "I got halfway to my dream, and then COVID happened. Not sure what the dream is now. I want to be a pilot. I still want to be a pilot." Ryan exercised his Career Imagination and made a plan; now he needs a new plan to get his dream back on track. He can do it. It will take way longer than he originally thought, but he can still be a pilot if he finds ways to keep the dream alive, finishes his schooling, and gets in his flight hours. There's likely to be a job for him since the pandemic not only derailed his schooling, but it also pushed a lot of older pilots into early retirement, adding to the already large number of boomer retirements, just like in many other fields.

Something similar happened to Donovan, who was laid off from a manufacturing and design internship at a car plant at the start of the pandemic. It's heartbreaking and demotivating to lose such a great opportunity, but there are still car design jobs waiting for Donovan, who has dreamed of cars since he was very little. "I have always had a passion for cars, studying them in detail all the way through my childhood. I want to design and build cars of various shapes and sizes and make them efficient and still beautiful. I love how something can look so simple and so straightforward, but behind it is so complex." Donovan needs a plan to get back in the game he knows he's made for.

Conclusion

If you've dreamed it and set a big goal, you need a path to get there. You don't have to get there in one step. Take the time to write it out, think about it, change it, adapt it, and fill it in. Just like a business plan, lay out where you're going, what you've got, what you need and how you'll get there. Include the kind of people you need and give yourself a chance for delays, mistakes, and detours. Don't forget to make time for some fun along the way.

Take Action

Do the following exercises and make notes in your Career Imagination Journal:

Do it today: Do a little research to find out where the jobs are and what skills you need to get them. This is the first step of your plan.

Do it tomorrow: Talk to someone in your field. Tell them you're looking for work and listen to what they think. This is an ongoing and crucial part of your plan.

Do it this month: Check in with yourself. Are you on track? Do you still believe? Do you need to do something new to keep yourself motivated?

A Final Note

Everyone deserves decent work, and enough of it. Our work must meet our needs and provide us with enough time off to live our lives, especially to spend time with family and in our communities. We should have the freedom to choose how, when, and where we work. And we all deserve the ongoing ability to go after higher-quality work, including self-employment, if that's what we want.

Most of us aren't born knowing what we want to do, although admittedly, a few are destined right from the start, and they know it. For the rest of us, we have to figure it out, and what we want changes over time anyway. It seems that just about every one of the many people we spoke with ended up somewhere they hadn't expected. And often, it was somewhere delightful. Okay, well, work is still work, but it *is* delightful to be doing work that is challenging, fulfilling, meaningful, *and* pays properly. This can look like so many different things, and maybe some things you haven't thought of.

I hope that this book has provided you with some inspiration to dream big. And that playing around in your own Career Imagination is a satisfying and fruitful pursuit. I hope that along the way, you keep doing what you really want to be doing so that even if you aren't getting paid for it today or paid enough, you will be tomorrow.

This comes more easily with a plan — a plan unique to you — with a few steps laid out in order, leading to your dream. And if it's a good plan, that something will be the right thing.

Good luck and best wishes for the job of your dreams. May you meet the right people along the way and enjoy the journey. I wish you good work and plentiful work. I wish you decent work.

About the Author

Elizabeth is a lecturer and researcher studying who we are when we work and how we can be successful in that work. She trained as a researcher at University College London, where she earned a Masters of Social Science Research, with distinction.

She is from Victoria, a small city on the western edge of Canada, where not too much happens. She went to the University of British Columbia, where she eventually received two degrees, a BA in History and an MBA. In her work, Elizabeth has done strategic planning, project management, sustainability, partner relations, and communications for a variety of employers, including large public agencies. Eventually, she moved to the private sector as an independent management consultant for small businesses, communities, and social enterprises.

After a career in some ordinary places, and some extraordinary ones, like an inner-city high school and a couple of Olympic Games, she went on to be a full-time Lecturer in Business Communications at the Sauder School of Business, UBC, a Top Forty business school.

Elizabeth raised and supported two sons on her own. She is an ordinary woman from an ordinary place, who has had a career that has at times been difficult, even struggling, and at other times been quite extraordinary. She is now working on a career as an entrepreneur.

Notes

[i] The term "Career Imagination" comes from the work of Cohen, L., & Duberley, J. (2021). Making sense of our working lives: The concept of the Career Imagination. *Organization Theory, 2*(2), 26317877211004600.

[ii] *Note:* This chapter draws on the expertise of internationally recognized policy and research bodies including the International Labour Organization (ILO); the World Economic Forum (WEF); the US Bureau of Labor Statistics; the World Bank; as well as non-partisan private research organizations including McKinsey & Company and the Pew Research Center.

[iii] Kochhar, Rakesh, "Which U.S. Workers Are More Exposed to AI on Their Jobs?" Pew Research Center, July 26, 2023, https://www.pewresearch.org/social-trends/2023/07/26/which-u-s-workers-are-more-exposed-to-ai-on-their-jobs/ and Wynoch, R., The Next Wave of Canada's Labour Market, CD Howe, 2020.

[iv] Kelly, J. (2021). Apple Employees Wrote a Letter to CEO Tim Cook Saying Why They Don't Want to Return to The Office. Retrieved on June 14, 2022, from https://www.forbes.com/sites/jackkelly/2021/06/05/apple-employees-wrote-a-letter-to-ceo-tim-cook-saying-why-they-dont-want-to-return-to-the-office/?sh=1acbcdbe6418

[v] Standing, G. (2011). The precariat: the new dangerous class. London: Bloomsbury Academic.

[vi] World Economic Forcum (2024), *Future of Jobs Report 2024.* https://www.weforum.org/publications/the-future-of-jobs-report-2020/in-full/2-3-emerging-and-declining-skills/

[vii] Furr, Nathan. "New Year Doubts? How To Overcome Self Doubt," Forbes, Jan 16, 2024.

Index

www.ingramcontent.com/pod-product-compliance
Lightning Source LLC
Chambersburg PA
CBHW042117190326
41519CB00030B/7526